Making Peace with CONFLICT

Mennonite Conciliation Service

Making Peace with Conflict is a project of Mennonite Conciliation Service (MCS), Akron, Pennsylvania.

MCS is a program of Mennonite Central Committee, U.S., whose purpose is to equip people to respond redemptively to interpersonal and systemic conflicts in our families, communities, congregations, and world.

MCS and its network of practitioners provide conflict resources, training, and intervention, including mediation, facilitation, and group consulting.

For more information, contact:

Mennonite Conciliation Service
21 South 12th St., P.O. Box 500
Akron, PA 17501-0500
717-859-3889
717-859-3875 fax
MCS@mccus.org
www.mennonitecc.ca/mcc/regions/united-states/mcs.html

Making Peace with CONFLICT

Practical
Skills
for
Conflict
Transformation

Edited by
**Carolyn Schrock-Shenk
and Lawrence Ressler**

Foreword by **Noel Santiago**
Introduction by **Nancy Heisey**

Herald
Press

Scottdale, Pennsylvania
Waterloo, Ontario

Library of Congress Cataloging-in-Publication Data
Making peace with conflict: practical skills for conflict transformation /
edited by Carolyn Schrock-Shenk and Lawrence Ressler; foreword by
Noel Santiago and introduction by Nancy Heisey.
      p. cm.
      Includes bibliographical references.
      ISBN 0-8361-9127-7 (alk. paper)
      1. Conflict management—Religious aspects—Christianity. 2. Conflict
management—religious aspects—Mennonites. I. Schrock-Shenk, Carolyn,
1955- II. Ressler, Lawrence, 1954- .
BV4597.53C58M34 1999
253'.7—dc21
99-22053

MAKING PEACE WITH CONFLICT
Copyright © 1999 by Herald Press, Scottdale, Pa. 15683
        Published simultaneously in Canada by Herald Press,
        Waterloo, Ont. N2L 6H7. All rights reserved
Library of Congress Catalog Number: 99-22053
International Standard Book Number: 0-8361-9127-7
Printed in the United States of America
Book and cover design by Gwen M. Stamm

12 11 10 09   10 9 8 7 6 5

To order or request information please call 1-800-245-7894 or visit
www.heraldpress.com.

To
Dave, Caleb, and John,
who are enormously patient with me. —Carolyn

To my family:
Sharon, Daniele, Stephanie, and Jake,
who have taught me so much about conflict, especially how
much I have to learn; and to my parents, who gave me a firm
place to stand. —Lawrence

Contents

Foreword

My first encounter with the field of conflict came in the early 1980s. I was working at Mennonite Central Committee, Akron, Pennsylvania. Ron Kraybill had been invited to lead a workshop for office staff on managing conflicts. How odd, I thought! Could conflicts be managed? What was this about? Would there be any practical application?

This turned out to be a tremendous stretching time for me. Ron talked about using "I-messages," "paraphrasing" as a way to ensure that true understanding had taken place, and more.

I remember several responses, especially one that went something like this: "Ron, this is all well and good, but I don't see the value for daily living. It's too mechanical and will come across to people as unreal."

Ron responded along these lines: "If I hear your concern correctly, you believe using these 'methods' might appear to others like we're not being genuine in our relationships with them. And it just doesn't feel quite right to you. Did I hear you right?"

The questioner nodded and sat down, satisfied to have made the point. Then that person and all of us realized what had just happened. We broke into laughter. Ron pointed out that he had been practicing these skills the entire time he had been with us. He noted that yes, they might at first feel mechanical or uncomfortable. But as we practiced using them, they would become second nature.

I was hooked. There was something about this conflict management that had a ring of truth. Since then I've found what Ron said to be true. It hasn't always been easy, and being Hispanic I've had to work at expressing the principles in a variety of forms shaped by diverse cultural contexts. Nevertheless, the basic skills I learned that day have held up in "real" life.

Carolyn Schrock-Shenk and Lawrence Ressler have done us a great service by pulling together this book. The many contributors bring to the subject depth and breadth that is biblically grounded, practical, and sensitive to a wide range of perspectives. Whether this is the first time you're encountering these concepts or you're a seasoned veteran, *Making Peace with Conflict* offers something for everyone.

Readers will discover that although skills are crucial, they're not enough. As believers, we need to call on the transforming power of God's Spirit in working with people, processes, and problems involved in conflict.

The contributors cover a range of topics: from basic skills in conflict transformation to power issues; from identity and race issues to global conflict. In true analytical form, the authors break down the parts and put them back together so we can better understand them. Their analyses and definitions convey a framework for understanding conflict even as they allow for openness in methods and forms. They will also stimulate discussion among holders of diverse views of conflict.

Making Peace with Conflict is virtually a conflict manual providing basic steps for addressing issues. Small groups, Sunday school classes, and cell/home groups will find it valuable both as a study tool and as a guide for addressing conflicts in their own settings. The book will help those uncomfortable with conflict as well as persons who have worked in difficult situations. Also acknowledged, however, is the likelihood that in many situations more skilled facilitators will be needed.

The book is easy to read—yet deep. Each chapter opens with a brief biography of the contributing author(s). Next comes a personal story or illustration, packed with power and insight, which introduces the concepts to follow. Helpful questions at the end of each chapter promote dialogue. There are also action steps and tables.

I encourage all of us to read reflectively, mining not only the many practical how-to's but also being stirred to reflect on our past experiences with conflict situations. As we do, we'll recall times we handled conflict well—and times we certainly didn't!

Readers will be affirmed, provoked, challenged, stretched. May God multiply the impact of this work so many persons will come to a deeper understanding of and commitment to God's call to peacemaking in a broken world.

—*Noel Santiago*
Mennonite Board of Missions Evangelism and Church Development
Franconia Mennonite Conference Consultant for Missions
Souderton, Pennsylvania

Editors' Preface

One of my (Lawrence's) most memorable conflict experiences took place when I was about thirteen. I made money mowing lawns for neighbors in a small central Ohio town. Once I took my push mower to a customer's home and found another boy about to mow the lawn. I informed him I'd been hired to do the mowing. He said he'd been hired. The woman wasn't home.

Since I had mowed the lawn before and was sure I'd been promised the job, I repeated kindly but firmly that the lawn was mine to mow. Before I knew what was happening, the boy drew back his fist. Hitting me squarely on the jaw, he knocked me to the ground.

After a few seconds I stood. I reacted in a manner I thought consistent with the teachings of Christ and true to my Mennonite heritage. Turning my face a bit, to expose the other cheek, I said, "Here, do you want to hit this side, too?"

The boy drew back and slugged me again. Falling to the ground a second time, I lay in a state of emotional and theological shock. Turning the other cheek hadn't generated the results I was hoping for. No one had told me what to do after turning the cheek. I got up, went to my lawn mower, and pushed it home, disappointed that I hadn't gotten my money and confused by the conflict.

Another fifteen years passed before I learned that peacemaking includes practical skills applicable to conflict. I was inspired as I went through the mediation training led by Ron Kraybill and John Paul Lederach of Mennonite Conciliation Service. Peacemaking was more than registering (as I had) as a conscientious objector. There was more to be done than turn the other cheek. It is actually possible to change conflict dynamics so peace can emerge from tension without harm being done.

Subsequent experiences as a social worker, family counselor, mediator, and regular churchgoer—but mostly over twenty years as husband and then father—have led me to conclude that conflict is everywhere.

Yet I have also come to see that conflict is not necessarily bad. Conflict, like anger, can result in good or ill. It can separate people; it can also bring people together. The goal of a peacemaker is not absence of conflict. Rather, the aim is to help people transform conflict from what separates to what unites.

Of course to say something is possible is not to suggest it is easy. During a recent phone call, a colleague in the conflict transformation field and I (Carolyn) discussed the work we have chosen and effects on our lives. He asked, "Have you ever wondered why so many in this field have had so much difficulty in their own relationships?" He was recently divorced.

Having struggled at points in my own marriage and my family of origin, I replied, "Yes, I have wondered. But I have no answers."

Indeed, one would think that those of us immersed in the whys and hows of conflict and conflict transformation should at a minimum practice what we know in our own lives. Alas, that doesn't necessarily follow. I for one regularly struggle with this question: How can I do my work—training, mediating, consulting, and developing resources related to conflict—with integrity when I have so much difficulty practicing what I know and preach?

Many times I've said to myself, "I'm not the person to do this work." Occasionally I've said this to a few trusted others. One friend, after listening attentively to my lament, responded, "You're precisely the person to do this work. You know how hard it is."

Indeed I do. I have my share of conflicts. I have my share of difficulty working through some of them. But I've discovered I'm not alone. I've also learned that neither the reality of conflicts nor of the intense struggle around some of them is cause for concern or embarrassment—precisely the opposite. The lack of conflict or struggle amid difficult conflicts is much more cause for concern.

So I began humbly this endeavor of writing and editing about conflict. There is nothing more important than "walking the talk," and I have far to go in doing so. Yet I took the project on confidently. I brought my experience to this task with the assurance that I am not alone. As an Anabaptist Christian, I join a host of others engaged in open, honest, and sometimes painful exploration of what it means to be a practical peacemaker in all of life.

We are grateful to the many who have been instrumental in bringing this book to fruition. Thanks go first and foremost to Michael A. King, the Pandora Press U.S. editor who was flexible and good-humored through it all. Thanks are also due the other seventeen chapter writers who wrote freely out of their experience and must have wondered if they would ever actually see it in print.

Readers of the manuscript provided us with valuable feedback. We are indebted to Wilma Bailey, Alice Price, Marcus Smucker, Luzdy Stucky, Cheryl Swartley, Velma Swartz, Valerie Weaver-Zercher, Alistair McKay, and the class at Eastern Mennonite University taught by Ron Kraybill. Finally, we are deeply grateful to Ed Nyce, who was invaluable during the project's final stages.

As editors and writers we have prayed for the presence of the Spirit of God during the journey through this book. We pray the same for you as reader. We hope you will engage these ideas and suggestions with good energy, agreeing or disagreeing openly, honestly, and in a constant search for that Truth always greater than our own.

—*Carolyn Schrock-Shenk*
Akron, Pennsylvania, and
Lawrence Ressler
Rochester, New York

Introduction

The Bible is not a textbook about conflict resolution. Yet when conflict has simmered or erupted among believers, whether in congregations, families, or communities, they have often tried to apply biblical principles to dealing with disagreements large and small. Traditionally, Mennonite Christians in conflict may have been most attracted to such biblical statements as these: "A soft answer turns away wrath," or "Do not let the sun go down on your anger," or "Vengeance is mine, I will repay, says the Lord."

Making Peace with Conflict is a good book for everyone who has lived with conflict or has lacked time for lengthy courses or academic reading related to conflict. It is also a book for those of us who have been enlivened and renewed by the biblical story of God's love affair with the universe and the contentious humans God placed on a tiny planet at the edge of one galaxy. As that big picture has taken shape in our understanding, we have also been able to learn new things from the Bible's many small stories of human beings—created in God's image, fallen into fighting, yet reaching out for renewed relationship with our Creator, human companions, and the world.

This book does not set out to offer a systematic study of biblical theology or conflict doctrine. Rather, in slim, readable, and carefully grouped chapters it offers the information needed by anyone seeking skills for living through the next conflict in more hopeful and healthy ways. Throughout the book, a host of biblical images and stories are called into the conversation. These underline the importance of that collection of holy stories for the writers in this volume, who seek to transform their own deep experiences with conflict through responses reflecting the divine image present in human beings.

The writers of the opening section point out approaches that challenge much common wisdom surrounding what it means to clash with others. Conflict is natural, claims Carolyn Schrock-Shenk. Almost imperceptibly she weaves in the first biblical story, the creation account

17

given in the first chapter of Genesis. Before describing humanity's fall out of relationship with God and each other, this great liturgy proclaims as good God's bringing forth difference—day and night, water and land, sun and moon, fish and birds, wild and domestic animals, and human beings as male and female.

Important to being truly human and truly Christian, adds Larry Dunn, is claiming our identity as part of the new creation by dealing wholesomely with differences and resulting conflicts. Here too biblical stories provide color. For Dunn, the tale of Cain and Abel exemplifies wrong ways to deal with difference. Regina Shands Stoltzfus reflects on the meaning of the cultural matrix in which all humans exist. She addresses the New Testament account of Peter finally "getting it" that he could share the good news with the Gentile Cornelius. Here she sees a case study of right ways to work through conflicts growing out of diversity.

Kori Leaman-Miller tells of a child who said after a waitress had encouraged him to give his own order, "She thinks I'm real." In her chapter emphasizing the central principle of listening amid conflict, Leaman-Miller later quotes the advice of James about being quick to listen and slow to speak. Meanwhile, Valerie Weaver-Zercher sees speaking as playing a powerful and creative role in conflict transformation. In making her case Weaver-Zercher returns to the beginning biblical account portraying God's word as the source of all that has been created.

Dalton Reimer calls for developing the skills of dialogue. These begin by acknowledging the existence of the Other and, when practiced well, lead to new understandings for both parties. Both Jesus and the Samaritan woman found such new understandings when Jesus risked entering the gap between them by requesting a drink. The power of stories to stir both profound teaching and learning, a power felt throughout the book, evokes the claims of Stanley Hauerwas that stories are necessary not because of their point but because they offer insights into truth not available by other means.[1]

In the section that proposes practical problem-solving strategies amid conflict, biblical wisdom enhances the counsel presented. Jesus' warning to get rid of the big piece of wood in one's own eye before trying to deal with the splinter in another's eye assists Dean Peachey's discussion about willingness to allow self-transformation through conflict.

Lawrence Ressler points out that Solomon, the biblical figure most noted for wisdom, is portrayed not as independently wise but as feeling in need of divine insight. John Powell underlines that the call to forgiveness even by one deeply wronged is founded in the Christian mandate for reconciliation expressed by the Apostle Paul. The fear which often pushes conflict over the edge into violence, advises Ann Shenk Wenger, finds an antidote in love. This principle is clearly articulated in John's first letter: "There is no fear in love, but perfect love casts out fear."

Thorny matters of power and of how differing levels of power promote conflict are addressed in three chapters. That from the earliest records the Bible understands and judges the human quest for power is highlighted by Iris de Leon-Hartshorn. She cites the temptation of Eve and Adam to be like God and the intercepted drive of the Babel Tower builders to reach the heavens. Angel Rafael Ocasio and Tobin Miller Shearer use that foundation to talk of how unequal power pushes prejudice into racism. Going beyond the stark understanding of human failure which the Bible does not ignore, Elaine Enns and Ched Myers insist on the underlying biblical theme of commitment to equality.

In a final section on applications of conflict transformation principles, Lorraine and Jim Stutzman Amstutz use the story of the brothers Esau and Jacob to launch their reflections on conflict in the family. The New Testament difference between Hebrew- and Greek-speaking believers, and the Jerusalem Conference that dealt with the question of whether and how the Jewish Law applied to Gentile Christians, help to shape chapters on conflict in the congregation written by Richard Blackburn, David Brubaker, and Alistair McKay.

In a concluding reflection on bringing conflict transformation commitment and strategy into international settings, Gerald Shenk notes that the commitment to biblical peacemaking shaped leaders of the sixteenth-century Anabaptist movement such as Menno Simons. In this way the Bible set a direction that has continued to motivate descendants of that movement as they enter the twenty-first century.

Making Peace with Conflict will provide fruitful reading for individuals ready to learn new skills for changing how they live and perceive their world. Its format, including end-of-chapter discussion questions, further points toward small group use. As the above survey suggests, church Bible study groups and Sunday school classes will find value in using this book as the basis for their own further reflection and practice.

Leaders of such groups might wonder whether biblical materials throughout the chapters are cited as proof texts or whether their use reflects a foundational understanding of the authors. Thus it is noteworthy that, in the biblical understanding, both diversity and goodness lie at the heart of God's creation and are most frequently called as witness throughout the book. The teachings of and stories about Jesus are also often cited, especially Jesus' specific instructions in Matthew 18 for confronting one who has wronged another in the faith community.

The beauty of the biblical record, however, sustains the perspectives and approaches of *Making Peace with Conflict* in an even more foundational way, whether or not the contemporary writers are always aware of it. The text of the Bible itself is a witness to the process of transforming conflict, as its writers continue to confront and wrestle with understanding God's purpose through the centuries of its writing. Take the wars of King David, which in the earlier record of 1 Kings kept him too busy to build God's temple. These are understood by the later record of 1 Chronicles as an impediment to temple building because of their very bloodshed. Yet even before that historical corrective, Isaiah had broken into the debate to proclaim the divine vision for God's place of worship: the temple was to be a place where many peoples "shall beat their swords into plowshares, and their spears into pruning hooks."

Conflict among earliest followers of Jesus is openly portrayed in the New Testament. Indeed, the Bible includes both the record of a mutually satisfactory conference (Jerusalem Council, noted above and told of in Acts 15) to deal with rules for Gentile believers and Paul's more personal and less comfortable reaction to the ruling of the church's first leaders in Galatians 2. Despite sharp differences suggested by such texts, underlying both seems to be the memory of Jesus' words when he quoted another Isaiah text on God's vision for a world full of difference: "My house shall be called a house of prayer for all the nations."

The clashing and interweaving in the biblical record thus itself embodies transformed conflict. The goal of this process is that the underlying Word of God's love continually be proclaimed until all people, in all their diversity, know that love and thus truly belong to God's realm.

—*Nancy R. Heisey*
  Instructor in Biblical Studies and Church History
  Eastern Mennonite University
  Harrisonburg, Virginia

FOUNDATIONS OF CONFLICT TRANSFORMATION

EXPERTS WOULD DEFINE CONFLICT something like this: conflict is a disagreement between interdependent people; it is the perception of incompatible or mutually exclusive needs or goals.[1] Put more simply, conflict equals differences plus tension. It is the tension we experience when a difference is discovered. There are three important elements in any conflict: people, problems, and process. Any of these can be at the root of a conflict. All are present in the progression and resolution of conflict.[2]

The people element of conflict refers to the "who" in a conflict. It includes those who are primarily involved in the conflict and most often visibly expressing it. It also includes those who are less visible but key to the conflict, those who get drawn in as it escalates, and those touched or affected by the fallout of the conflict. This element also includes the relationships involved. What is the nature of those relationships? Where has there been hurt or brokenness? What are the strengths on which reconciliation can be built?

Problems refers to the "what" of conflict. It involves the specific issues around which people differ. A critical and devastating escalation in a conflict can take place when the focus on issue as problem shifts to focus on people as problem. A vital goal in moving through conflict is to understand the concerns and needs beneath the particular position that each participant brings. What really matters to them? This is often where common ground is found and seeds of resolution to the problem can be planted and nurtured.

Process refers to the "how" of a conflict, to the way decisions are made and problems addressed. Process is the most unrecognized cause of conflict and the most ignored element in addressing conflict. Frequently the process itself is the main problem. Generally people can live with a decision they may not actually prefer if they have had a voice in that decision or resolution. People who feel unable to influence the decisions that affect their lives will often not support or cooperate with the decisions. They may undermine them, either by openly defying the decisions or by subtly subverting them.

Feeling excluded leads to a sense of powerlessness, insignificance, and irrelevance. This is true for individuals as well as entire groups of people who are marginalized. Continued over a period of time, this sense will lead to cynicism and hopelessness. One of the keys to transforming conflict is to develop a process that gives a voice to all of the persons involved.

Conflict situations are typically complex. To better understand what is happening, it is helpful to ask some questions. With respect to people, it is useful to ask who is involved, what they are feeling and thinking, what their needs and perceptions are, and what they believe and value. Questions about the problem include what the issues between people are, what concrete concerns and differences will need to be resolved, which of the issues are primary and which tangential.

Finally, questions about the process need to be asked. What kind of process is occurring, how have things been decided so far, who has been making the decisions, who is being left out, how have things been communicated or not, how can the process best proceed to ensure safe participation of all?

In all of this, questions about power need to be addressed since power and conflict are always interrelated. What are the sources of power of those in the conflict? Is there a substantial power imbalance? How can the less powerful become more empowered? Is power being misused or abused? What does the interpersonal conflict tell us about the broader societal structures in terms of power and possible oppression?

Power and its use and abuse is always a significant factor when conflict goes awry or turns violent. When someone, or a group of someones, has been silenced or victimized, the conflict is no longer a neutral one or simply "differences with tension." It has become destructive and sometimes even lethal. The authors in Part Four begin to deal with these types of conflicts.

Part One of the book examines some of the foundational issues related to conflict transformation. Chapter 1 provides an overview of what conflict is, some key principles that are helpful to know about conflict, and a look at the way conflict has been viewed over the years. Chapter 2 explores the important area of identity in conflict. The tension we feel and the way we respond reflects who we are individually. Chapter 3 looks at the role of culture in conflict. The tensions individuals feel and the way they respond also reflect the assumptions, values, and patterns that the group has put into place.

Individuals influence the group, but the group also influences individuals. Transforming conflict requires attention to both aspects.

1

Introducing Conflict and Conflict Transformation

By Carolyn Schrock-Shenk

Carolyn Schrock-Shenk has had much conflict experience as wife of Dave and mother of Caleb in addition to roles as daughter, sister, friend, neighbor, co-worker, and church member. She is still learning to practice what she preaches. She has been working more formally with conflict since 1990 and since 1992 has been Mennonite Conciliation Service assistant director and director. In that capacity she does training, intervention, and resource development, including serving as editor of Conciliation Quarterly. *In spare time she loves to read, travel, play tennis, and go on family outings.*

Hurt and Alone

I was in third grade when in conflict I discovered a primal fear. I was sure my turn in a game had been skipped. I stated my opinion tentatively at first, then emphatically, but was ignored. I felt terribly hurt and rejected. For a long time—days or even weeks—I didn't play with my friends. I sat alone at recess on a rock culvert, immersed in loneliness, wishing I had the courage to rejoin my friends. But pride and fear held me back. I was too proud to admit how hurt I was and how much I cared and too afraid it didn't matter to them at all. I was alienated from some of the people who mattered most to me. The chords of relationship were for a time devastatingly broken.

Connectedness: The Essence of Life

The Essence of Life

Connectedness—to God and to that which God created—is the essence of life. It is the meaning for which we search, the food that nourishes our souls. Little compares to cuddling a sleepy child on one's shoulder, a walk in the woods when God is as present as the trees, the satisfaction of a heart-level conversation bathed with understanding.

Connectedness has to do with intimacy. It involves being known for who I really am and being all the more beloved by the other for that knowing. Once I received a letter from a friend facing difficulties. She believed she was no longer the person she had been. Her intense self-doubt was draining her energy and passion.

I wrote back saying I had no advice but I was glad I could listen. "Pam," I wrote, "I in no way want to minimize what you're experiencing. I believe you're truly going through a desolate wilderness. If you were here, I would want to listen more and let you spill out that vinegar in your blood. But you're not here and so I must respond with what's on my heart. I know you, Pam, and here is what I know you to be." Then I described the Pam I know and love, a picture different from either her current self-understanding as fundamentally flawed or her former self-understanding as superwoman.

Pam reported that my letter was a holy thing, that she heard the word of God in it, that she was grateful there was still enough of her around to recognize the holy when she saw it. She said, "I think the most important thing one person can say to another is 'I know you'—and that what follows that statement is actually much less significant than that one is known by another."

I believe Pam is right. Knowing is the essence of God's relationship with us. Psalm 139 describes this powerfully:

> O Lord, you have searched me and known me.
> You know when I sit down and when I rise up; you discern my thoughts
>   from far away.
> You search out my path and my lying down, and are acquainted with all
>   my ways.
> Even before a word is on my tongue, O Lord, you know it completely.
> You hem me in, behind and before, and lay your hand upon me.
> Such knowledge is too wonderful for me; it is so high that I cannot attain it.

The psalmist is known by God and has come to know God in return. "How precious to me are your thoughts, O God." It is through knowing that God and the psalmist are bonded.

The Potential in Conflict

Ironically, conflict is an opportunity to know. Without conflict we tend to keep ourselves carefully hidden from God and from others. While hiding we're often deaf to the voice of God and "protected" from new learning. Struggling through conflict can make us vulnerable, sharpen our senses, help us see our own inadequacy and narrow-mindedness, and open us to God and to others in new ways.

The Psalms make a clear connection between conflict and knowing. As the psalmist struggles, he spills out his lament, anger, accusations, and doubts, becoming transparent before God. One might think that the psalmist's conflicts and his honesty about them would destroy his relationship with God. Rather, they strengthen that bond of knowing as he comes to understand new truth and experiences God in fresh and powerful ways.

The same is true in human relationships. A big reason Pam and I have a deep friendship and know each other so well is that we have had considerable conflict. We disagree on issues. Our communication goes awry. We mistake each other's motives. In these conflicts we become more vulnerable and see things in the other that are kept well-hidden in easier times. Conflict has strengthened our relationship.

The Fear of Disconnectedness

If conflict can bring intimacy and connection, it can also alienate and tear apart, as in the first conflict recorded in Genesis 3. Forbidden fruit tempts Adam and Eve. I suspect there is agony between verses two and six as conflict brews inside and perhaps even between them. They eat the fruit, immediately realize their vulnerability, and hide from each other and God. In response to conflict, Adam and Eve choose the self-gratification which brings disconnection and pain.

We were created to be connected, both with God and with each other. We fear losing that connection when conflict bursts into our lives. We fear for good reason. The violence and sin both in and outside us defies connectedness and intimacy. It pushes us toward negative and destructive responses.

Conflict, in other words, can bring pain and violence and disconnection. Or it can bring surprising new growth and intimacy and understanding into our relationships.

Key Conflict Principles

The Staff at CO-HOPE

Decreasing funds forced CO-HOPE, a small, nonprofit organization, to cut programs. Downsizing is a difficult and conflict-filled process. The staff proceeded carefully. Under capable leadership they agreed first on how to make the decision, gather input from each person, collect needed information from outside sources, generate and weigh options. They agreed on discussion guidelines, such as respectful and nonjudgmental listening, speaking honestly for oneself, and communicating directly with each other when the going got tough rather than in the breakroom at "meetings after the meetings." Believing that rushing would have devastating long-term consequences, they also committed to a huge block of decision-making time.

The going was tough. There were many strong opinions. Often tension rose. But they hung together and finally reached a decision most felt good about and all were ready to live with. Although there was regret about what would be cut, and even criticisms about ways the decision-making process could have been better, the outcome was positive. Staff members had worked sensitively together, honored each other's input, and changed or modified their views along the way. Though exhausted, most moved on with a renewed sense that they were each a valued member of a good team. Overall, the conflict was constructive.

The Mt. Pleasant Congregation

The Mt. Pleasant congregation was different. There were strong theological differences regarding women in leadership and views of Scriptures as well as varied opinions about the quality of the pastor's leadership. Most discussions of these differences took place in the parking lot and behind closed doors. Genuine disagreement over issues was soon indistinguishable from the personal assaults and bitter recriminations that tumbled out of the frustrated members.

Over time, opposing sides gathered new members and issues and dug their heels deeper into their positions. By the time it was "over," nearly half of the families had left in bitterness. The problem at the Mt. Pleasant Church was not theological differences or opinions about the pastor; the problem was how people chose to respond to differences. Defensiveness, self-protection, desire to win, even readiness to wound others became the norm. Mt. Pleasant members were exhausted and wounded, spiritually and emotionally.

The conflicts experienced by these two groups differed in a variety of ways. Perhaps the most fundamental difference was in their basic attitudes and beliefs. The longer I work with people in conflict, the more I believe our ability to work through conflict successfully has much to do with the attitude we bring to it. How we view and feel about self, the other, conflict, truth, and even God often determines how we work with conflict.

Most of us need a fairly dramatic shift in our understanding of conflict. Several key principles have become pillars in my emerging understanding.

Conflict Is Natural

The first key principle is this: *Conflict is natural*. In the first line of *The Road Less Traveled*, M. Scott Peck says, "Life is difficult."[3] Peck's book essentially says, deal with it. Stop expecting otherwise. So too with conflict. Life is full of it. In fact, conflict is often what makes life difficult! While it is true that we can learn to avoid some of the unnecessary stuff, it is also true that learning how to deal well with conflict will not keep it out of our lives.

I'm reminded of my adjustment to Philippine weather during my years there with Mennonite Central Committee. People told me I would adjust to the eleven months of intense heat each year. I assumed, and fervently hoped, that adjustment meant I would perspire less. My sweat glands, however, were as prolific the second year as the first. What began to happen instead was that I noticed it less. My indispensable handkerchief became an automatic tool in my hand. Feeling hot and being sticky wet was no longer the primary—and sometimes only—thing on my mind. Perspiring no longer ruled or spoiled my day. It was simply part of the territory, and I coped successfully.

Conflict, like the Philippine heat, is simply part of the territory of life. Rather than trying to eliminate it, we must somehow make peace with its presence. Conflict need not control us or spoil our enjoyment of life. In fact, just as much good emerges out of that Philippine heat, so conflict handled with care can bring much good in our lives.

Our basic understanding of conflict is critical because it determines how we respond. If we believe conflict with spouse, coworker, or church family is unnatural, inappropriate, or wrong, then we become ashamed or embarrassed when we find ourselves in conflict situations. And when something is shameful or embarrassing, we generally try to avoid it, deny its presence, or do whatever we need to do to get through it fast. As a consequence, there is little motivation to learn healthy skills and processes for dealing with conflict. Why learn to deal constructively with something that shouldn't be happening in the first place?

The CO-HOPE staff and leadership understood that downsizing would produce conflict. They expected differences and tension and made plans to deal with them. The Mt. Pleasant congregation, on the other hand, denied their growing differences until they burst out of control. The path they each walked to deal with their conflicts had everything to do with their fundamental attitudes and beliefs about conflict.

Genesis 1 tells the creation story. Here is a diversification program *extraordinaire* culminating with the creation of two human beings blessed with the same diversity God has given the rest of creation. God also gives those beings free will. They can think for themselves and make choices. If there is a recipe for conflict, this is surely it. And just as surely, God knew it.

So perhaps it is fair to say that not only is conflict natural, but that it existed before evil and that Adam and Eve, given their differences and freedom of choice, had conflict. Since sin had not yet entered the world, their responses to those conflicts were collaborative, constructive, and positive. Perhaps sin and evil entered precisely when they chose a negative response to the conflict they encountered.[4]

Constructive or Destructive: It's Our Choice

A second key principle about conflict goes something like this: *We can't always choose the conflicts that come into our lives, but we can choose our responses to those conflicts.* Our response determines whether conflicts we encounter will be constructive or destructive; whether they will produce connection or alienation, whether they move us toward more justice and right relationships or toward more oppression, whether they lead us toward discovery and new truth or toward rigidity and narrowness. A comparison of some characteristics of constructive and destructive conflict is summarized in Table 1 (end of chapter).

The fact that there is conflict in my life merely says I am alive and well. The amount of conflict may say a bit more about me. It may point to the kind of job I have, the extent of my interactions with others, or even something about the nature of my personality. What says most about me is the quality of my conflicts and how I respond to them.

Contrary to how we may feel when in the midst of conflict, we can choose how to respond. We need not follow our first impulse nor the unhelpful patterns we may have learned from family or broader society. The notion that the devil (or anyone, for that matter) made me do it is a cop-out. No one makes us do anything.

A key to making constructive choices is to separate feelings from actions. Anger, resentment, jealousy, hurt, and fear are natural feelings when tension rises. They become wrong when we nurture them or act destructively on them. The actions we choose, not our spontaneous feelings, determine whether conflict will be constructive or destructive.

There are several key points to make regarding responses to conflict. First, a destructive response breeds more unnecessary and destructive conflict. For example, my choice to respond with judgment and accusation to my husband's unfinished project invites his defensiveness and escalates destructive conflict. Escalation will continue until one of us opts for more constructive responses. Like mushrooms in compost, more conflicts spring up out of resentment and decreasing trust.

Conversely, my choice to respond constructively, such as by expressing disappointment rather than judging, will likely not fuel that conflict or others. Instead, it will add the positive nutrients of understanding and empathy to the relationship soil, increasing the likelihood that we will also confront positively the next inevitable conflict.

Second, a host of factors can limit options for creative responses. Some face huge obstacles over which they have little control. For example, people of color (a phrase referring to indigenous peoples of North America and the diasporas of Africa, Asia, Latin America, and the Middle East) in a society that values whiteness have fewer options when they are viewed as less capable or trustworthy. Women have fewer options when they are expected to be silent and subservient. People with limited resources have fewer options when they are unable to meet basic needs. Children have fewer options because they may not be able to see beyond their immediate surroundings and the people closest to them. Amid such limitations, choosing constructive options remains possible but is more difficult.

Third, in situations of discrimination, oppression, or violence, even a constructive response will initially produce more tension and conflict. While this can be risky and frightening, we need to expect it and plan how to deal with it. This is true in interpersonal relationships. For example, the choice of an abused spouse to leave the other threatens the abuser, who may turn even more violent. Such increased tension does not mean leaving is a destructive response. Also in situations of systemic oppression, nonviolent organizing usually leads initially to more repression by the powerful. This increased conflict is to be expected.

The measure for whether a response is constructive is not whether conflict lessens. Rather, the criteria are whether the response moves the situation toward more justice and the people involved toward right and equal relationships.

A Part of the Truth

A third key principle is this: *In any conflict I have part, but only part, of the truth.* This is one of the most difficult principles to keep in mind amid conflict. We each bring our own perspective, our own lens, and it determines what we see. I frequently work with people in conflict and find myself thinking, "Someone is lying here; these stories are completely opposite." Indeed I do believe that at times people lie. More often, I discover they are not lying but simply describing what a situation has looked and felt like to them. And the very same experience has been perceived quite differently by another.

Many of us who experience conflict are likely to find that it takes enormous discipline to stay open to the reality that there is truth larger than our own understanding of it. First Corinthians 13 says that we only know in part (v. 9) and see through a mirror dimly (v. 12). Two concepts are equally important here. First, there is the part of the truth I have experienced. It is legitimate and valid; I have the right and responsibility to name it clearly and lovingly. The second equally important concept is that you, as my opponent in conflict, also have a valid and legitimate perspective on truth which you also must name. To have respectful dialogue and come to constructive understanding, we must hold these truths in tension—even if (or perhaps especially if) they are very different.

It is no accident that this need for humility or, as one friend calls it, the grace of uncertainty, comes in the middle of the famed "love chapter." It is all about love. I seek to love and listen to the other even as I love and listen to myself. We are both created in the image of God.

This does not mean that in all situations we each have equal parts of the truth. There are many situations of crime and oppression where one person's or group's perspective reigns and the perspective or experience of the other is given little or no credibility. This is true at a systemic level, such as racial discrimination, or at an interpersonal level, such as in situations of child abuse. Jesus' stand with the poor and powerless is a call to give legitimacy and credibility to those whose voices and experiences have not mattered to the same extent. This does not mean that in such conflicts we shut out the truth of the group in power or the perpetrator of abuse. Rather, it means that we lift up the experience of the oppressed and the victim. Only then can we begin justly to address the conflicts present in a situation.

Conflict's Bad Rap

If conflict itself is neutral, if it has both positive and negative potential, and if we all have part of the truth in conflict situations, why is our experience of it so often negative? When I ask people to describe or draw pictures of conflict, why do they mostly contain pain, bitterness, hostility, separation, revenge, even death? Why do those who do talk about conflict as positive often say it with a smile, or with the indication that this particular truth is a fairly recent acquisition? Why has conflict gotten such a bad rap? There are several interconnected reasons, stemming from common misperceptions.

If It's Successful, It Isn't Really Conflict

We often label as conflict only those situations which include such negative elements as bitterness, hurt, and division. We clearly see and name conflict at places like Mt. Pleasant. In such settings conflict is so real we may actually feel physically sick. However, in situations like the one at CO-HOPE, where there are few negative aspects, we hesitate to call the differences conflict. When the decision-making process is fairly healthy, we may not recognize the many and deep conflicts that are present and addressed.

Yet conflict with positive outcomes takes place all the time. It happens in big ways like deciding how to cut programs. It also happens in smaller ways. For example, my husband and I agreed, after intense conversation, to list and schedule the remaining renovation projects and how they would get completed. Similarly my son and I negotiated our disagreement over the timing and amount of his next candy fix, again with much discussion as well as some cajoling. My coworker and I regularly divide tasks neither of us enjoys.

These are all conflicts, managed with relative ease and resulting in constructive ends. Our perception of conflict can change dramatically when we begin to recognize the times we work with or through disagreement successfully.

If It Hurts, It's Bad

Most of us see pain and struggle as only negative. We try to avoid situations which may lead to feeling hurt. Tension or an angry exchange leads us to conclude something is awry. Many of us have been taught that "negative" emotions such as anger, fear, hurt, and jealousy are inherently problematic. So we try to avoid them.

Conflict, however, is rarely neat and nice or full of warm, fuzzy feelings. There is much about conflict that is just plain messy, chaotic, and anxiety-filled. It doesn't matter how skilled we are or how pure our intentions: we still deal with feelings of awkwardness, anger, competitiveness, and suspicion.

Often the presence of these reactions has led us to believe conflict is negative precisely because it gives rise to such feelings. Rather than understanding that these are normal reactions amid which we can choose positive actions, we have determined that their existence means God is neither present nor pleased when there is conflict.

Conflict Is Sin

Many of us have been taught God is absent in conflict. We have often worked to achieve a false unity based on uniformity of thought and action rather than on oneness of spirit. This belief has devastated relationships and congregations. It has closed down emotions, honest expression, and dialogue about differences. It has often led us to speak and act as if we have the complete truth. Then we become insecure and suspicious when faced with differing beliefs or opinions.

Differences are to be expected, acknowledged, and affirmed. Conflict opens us to new truth and understanding. Try taking all the conflicts out of the Bible, our book of truth. What remains is a skinny volume indeed. If we truly believe this we can begin to understand conflict settings as holy ground, as places where God is present in powerful ways, as opportunities to gain new insight and understanding. Imagine how different our conflicts would be if we could move from an "Oh dear, how terrible" to "What is God trying to say to us?"

Dealing with conflict constructively takes us another step forward in maturity. We begin to see conflict in a more positive light—even if it brings pain or immense challenges.

It's Easy To Be At Peace

Living peaceably through conflicts ought to be easy, we sometimes think. Rodney King's words after the Los Angeles rebellion in 1992—"Can't we just all get along?"—live on and strike a chord with many of us. Because we are not prepared for the complexity of conflict, we have not given sufficient attention to equipping ourselves for the task of conflict transformation and peacemaking. We have often equated it with equally huge tasks like parenting, assuming that our good sense and good will can carry us through.

Such thinking is, however, blind to the true challenges we face. In the absence of intentional learning we have picked up society's "fight, flee, or sue" responses to conflict. Because fighting or suing has seemed counter to belief in "turning the other cheek," the church has often taught us to flee, to avoid conflict, to repress our needs and feelings, to reject our differences. We have seldom been taught how to be proactive in conflict and to understand that conflict transformation is a deeply spiritual task that demands commitment, discipline, new skills, much practice, and constant vigilance from each of us.

What's Our Goal in Conflict?

Over the years the goals of conflict practitioners have changed. This has been reflected in changes in the terminology used by practitioners.[5]

Conflict Resolution

Experts in the field of conflict first coined the phrase *conflict resolution*. Such language promotes the need to finish conflict, to wrap it up and put it behind. Resolution may even imply absence or elimination of conflict as the goal. The problem with this view is that it is rarely possible nor desirable to completely close up a conflict even when we resolve specific pieces of it. Furthermore, we do not want to eliminate conflict. It is precisely in the struggle of conflict, in the memories of the struggle, and in ongoing relationship tensions that we learn and grow.

Conflict Management

Sometime later, the term *conflict management* emerged. This implies a goal of "keeping the lid on." Attempts are made to keep conflict and the expression of conflict within "acceptable" parameters. For example, we may try not to raise our voice or get too angry.

The problem with this approach is the attempt to keep things nice on the surface when deeper issues must be addressed. Many times we need to get angry and raise our voices, literally or figuratively, to bring the conflict to light. Conflict management also raises the question of who sets the standards or acceptable parameters.

In addition, conflict management implies that conflict follows predictable patterns. It suggests that if we understand those patterns we can control, direct, and manipulate the course of conflict. This is partly true, as much of the discussion in this book will suggest; it is also inadequate. Human beings are so much more than predictable patterns that can and should be manipulated.

Conflict Transformation

More recently, many in the field have begun to refer to the goal as *conflict transformation*. This approach more accurately describes what happens in conflict and what we want to have happen. Resolution focuses mostly on the "problem" dimension of conflict, finding resolution to the actual issues. Management focuses on the "process" dimension, finding ways to work though conflict. Though we seek change in all three dimensions of conflict, the notion of transformation begins with and focuses more heavily on the people involved and on their relationships with each other.

Conclusion

For people in conflict, Baruch Bush and Folger in *The Promise of Mediation* maintain that one goal of transformation is empowerment. When in conflict, we are often "weak," meaning confused, fearful, and unsure of what to do. Our goal is to move toward becoming less anxious, clearer, more confident, more organized. We need to regain a sense of strength, of being able to act to handle life's problems. We need to become, in other words, empowered.[6]

A second equally important goal, say Baruch Bush and Folger, is recognition. When in conflict we are self-absorbed, defensive, suspicious, and incapable of seeing beyond ourselves to the needs and interests of another. Transformation, then, includes moving from self-absorption to recognition; to being more open, attentive, and responsive to the perspective and situation of another.

These two goals, empowerment and recognition, describe in secular terms the essentially spiritual goals of conflict. I seek to "love my neighbor as myself." This means I love myself and listen deeply to my own heart; to my feelings, needs, hopes, values, commitments; to the very Spirit of God in me. I become empowered. Likewise, I seek to love and listen deeply to the heart of the other and the Spirit of God in the other. I recognize the other. Neither of these are easy tasks in the presence of conflict, precisely because we tend to be weak and self-absorbed, unable to hear our own hearts or the heart of the other.

Squarely in the midst of those tendencies, however, lies the powerful transformative potential of conflict.

Discussion Questions

1. When you think of conflict, what comes to mind? Is the definition "differences plus tension" a good one? Why or why not?

2. This chapter suggests that conflict is natural, even a result of God's good creation. How do you respond?

3. Think of a conflict. What response choices did you have? Were you aware of choices? If you could do it over, what might you change?

4. Conflict is presented as sometimes constructive. Can you think of examples? If the conflict was destructive, what made it so? Could it have become constructive if handled differently?

5. What is your attitude toward conflict? How does it affect the way you deal with it?

6. Is conflict transformation a realistic goal? How does it differ from management or resolution? Does it change how you handle conflict?

Table 1: Characteristics of Conflict

Characteristics Of Constructive Conflicts	Characteristics Of Destructive Conflicts
• People change, adjust, compromise	• People are rigid, inflexible, insistent
• People interact with an intent to learn instead of an intent to protect.	• People interact with the intent to protect self and hurt the other
• People do not stay stuck in a conflict; conflicts move and change	• People become stuck in, and defined by, a particular conflict
• Increased self-esteem in the participants.	• Increased fear, anger and insecurity
• Increased motivation for positive connection with others	• "Fight pattern" (desire to destroy the other's argument or their person) or "flight pattern" (avoidance, resentment, triangling)
• Parties have a relationship focus	• Parties only look out for their own self interests
• Presence of empathy	• Presence of demeaning verbal and non-verbal communication
• Primarily cooperative, marked by egalitarian relationships	• Primarily competitive and destructive, marked by domination and subordination patterns

Drawn from Joyce Hocker and William Wilmot, *Interpersonal Conflict*, 4th ed. (Madison, Wis. William C. Brown Communication, 1978), 32-38

2

Transforming Identity in Conflict

by Larry A. Dunn

Larry Dunn is a mediator and trainer for Mennonite Central Committee in Labrador, Canada. He lives with his wife Susan and their three sons, Seth, Eli and Isaac. As a nonethnic member of the Mennonite Church, he has found that the Anabaptist tradition feels like home and provides a community in which to pursue his calling as peacemaker. His time living and working in Fresno and Pasadena, California; Philadelphia, Pennsylvania; Syracuse, New York; and now Labrador has enriched his appreciation for the different ways people address conflict. Of special interest to him is the experience of Native Americans and Aboriginal Peoples of Canada.

Richard's Remorse

Richard, a respected elder in the church, sat with head in hands, quietly sobbing. He spoke softly but just loud enough that everyone in the room could hear his question. "What have I become?" he asked. "This conflict has made me someone I'm not proud of."

Richard's reflection had come at the end of a long meeting in which he and others wrestled with long-simmering church conflict. People had been hurt, some deeply. A few had left the congregation. All had been affected. Like Richard, many had treated others in ways they now regretted. Richard's harmful behavior was uncharacteristic. This was not the "real" Richard, the respected church elder people had always known. He had become someone different.

Identity and Conflict

What we disagree about raises questions of who we are and who we want to become. In other words, conflict is related to identity. The things we care about most deeply are likely to engage us in the greatest conflict. When conflict strikes at the core of who we are and may become, it can profoundly affect us. It can even transform our entire religious, social, or cultural group for generations to come.

The example of Richard shows how one individual can be affected by conflict. In more extreme cases, ethnic groups clash over which people are the legitimate cultural bearers of a national identity. Sometimes they change or even create "traditions" to support their cause. Among several North American religious denominations, members hotly debate what it may mean to accept women, persons of color, or gays and lesbians into their church and leadership roles. Whether viewed with a sense of hope or fear, the tension around these changes is related to identity.

Jesus' Identity in Conflict

In Mark's account of Jesus' life and ministry, we find Jesus asking his disciples an important question of identity: "Who do people say that I am?" he asked them. "Who do you say that I am?" (8:27, 29a).

Before asking these questions, Jesus had already been at the center of religious and social conflict. Jesus had claimed power to forgive sins (Mark 2:5). He had been held in contempt for eating among sinners and tax collectors (2:16). He had been conspired against for violating Sabbath laws (2:24; 3:6) and disregarding the tradition of the elders (7:5). Rumors had swirled about him following the murder of John the Baptist (6:14).

All of these events, filled with conflict, raised questions about who this man from Nazareth really was. "Who can forgive sins but God alone?" (2:7b), they asked. "Is not this the carpenter, the son of Mary..." (6:3a)? Undoubtedly, some of his disciples and followers were beginning to wonder what they were getting into, who *they* were becoming. Indeed, many had witnessed and experienced personal transformation and healing through Jesus' ministry.

Our Many Selves

The connection between identity and conflict is complex because who we are is shaped by the many roles and relationships in our lives. I am a husband, a father, a son, and a brother. I am a white, middle-class male of mixed European heritage who is a nonethnic member of a particular Christian tradition (Mennonite). I am also a citizen of one country (the United States) who presently lives in another country (Canada) amid a significant Native population. Each role and relationship is influenced by the existence of the others.

Each of these aspects of myself, and many more, have shaped and continue to affect who I am. They also contribute to my opinions and provide the "stuff" of conflict in my life. Sometimes I experience conflict with others simply because I am male and see things from that point of view. Sometimes conflict is related to my perspective as father, Mennonite, European-American, or person living a middle-class lifestyle.

To make matters more complicated, our individual and collective "selves" are always changing. People and groups grow older, and their perspectives change. Roles and relationships change throughout life. The environment around us changes.

By definition, social conflict involves other people. The boundaries of my self are overlapping and integrated with the boundaries of others around me. Whether you are a friend, neighbor, or kin, who I am is intertwined with who you are. In conflict, my individual identity will encounter your identity. Conflict forms and re-forms our selves because we are separate *from* and yet connected *to* others. Conflict, in other words, is an inevitable and normal part of these circumstances.

The Church and Conflict

Contrary to the commonly held notion that the church should be conflict-free, the church by its nature will be drawn into the business of dealing with conflicts. Jesus is recorded as using the term "church" (*ekklesia*) only twice, in Matthew 16:18 and 18:17. In fact, these are the only two uses of the term in all four Gospels. In the eighteenth chapter of Matthew's account, we find Jesus dealing with the disciples' bickering over power and prestige (1-5), a parable about the restoration of lost souls (10-14), and a process for bringing about the forgiveness of sins (15-35).

In one of the two places that Jesus chooses to discuss the identity of the church, conflict is the main topic! We might rightly conclude that *the church is being the church when dealing with conflict.* If our calling is to live out the reality that Christ has broken down false walls and ended the hostility between all people (Gal. 3:28; Eph. 2:14), then who we are as Christians is defined by how we deal with conflict.

The radical approach to conflict for Christians is found in the Sermon on the Mount.

> "You have heard that it was said, 'An eye for an eye and a tooth for a tooth.' But I say to you, Do not resist an evildoer. But if anyone strikes you on the right cheek, turn the other also; and if anyone wants to sue you and take your coat, give your cloak as well; and if anyone forces

you to go one mile, go also the second mile. Give to everyone who begs from you, and do not refuse anyone who wants to borrow from you.

"You have heard that it was said, 'You shall love your neighbor and hate your enemy.' But I say to you, Love your enemies and pray for those who persecute you, so that you may be children of your Father in heaven; for he makes his sun rise on the evil and on the good, and sends rain on the righteous and on the unrighteous. For if you love those who love you, what reward do you have? Do not even the tax collectors do the same? And if you greet only your brothers and sisters, what more are you doing than others? Do not even the Gentiles do the same? Be perfect, therefore, as your heavenly Father is perfect." (Matt. 5:38-48)

Followers of Christ need to be aware of the ways in which conflict can transform lives, for better and for worse. We must prepare ourselves as best we can to be agents of conflict transformation, engaging conflict to further the work of God's kingdom in all people's lives.

Aspects of Identity and Conflict

Who I Am Shapes Conflict

As a member of the Mennonite church, I have been adopted into a group with a tradition of dealing with conflict in nonviolent and peaceful ways. When I share this commitment with other Christians outside that tradition, I am often asked, "What would you do if. . . ?" This is usually posed as a hypothetical situation involving an intruder in my house or someone threatening to assault my wife or children.

My answer usually surprises them. "I don't know what I would do," I say, half-spoiling their expectation that I will respond with the kind of certainty easily refuted. While I cannot say for sure what I would do in every situation, I can tell them what I hope I would do. I hope my response would be shaped by my commitment to not harm another human being, even while trying to prevent my wife or children from being harmed.

I believe all Christians are called to be peacemakers. I don't always fulfill that commitment in every way I might, but I try to allow it to shape what I do with my life. At times it has prevented me from truly harming others. The kind of person I am shapes my experience of conflict and how I deal with it. I have learned, for example, to see many conflicts as an opportunity for growth and creative problem solving. I have become more skillful than I once was by participating in workshops and taking the risk of entering into conflict with others despite my fear.

Conflict Shapes Who I Am

Conflict also has the power to shape who we are and how we live, individually and collectively. In my work with Mennonite Central Committee as a mediator in Canada, I have seen how the lives of Labrador's Native people have been profoundly changed by involvement in conflicts with other Native and non-Native people. In many cases stresses over forced settlement and assimilation have resulted in loss or near-loss of traditional practices thousands of years old.

As Native groups fight and negotiate for the right to maintain these traditional activities, much of the resources of both time and money that could be used for hunting and living in the country are instead spent engaging opponents in court and elsewhere. Fortunately, some have dealt with such challenges by returning to the very practices they feel are threatened. Many find healing and strength through the spiritual renewal that comes from living off the land.

Conflict affects us deeply, especially when we feel that our sense of safety, control, recognition, or our very existence is threatened. Paradoxically, even as we engage in efforts to maintain these essential aspects of who we are, those very efforts are already at work shaping who we will become in the future.

Ways of Relating to the "Other": Exclusion and Embrace[7]

Excluding the Other

There are at least two ways of dealing with those with whom we find ourselves in conflict. The first is to exclude the other. One way to exclude is to label the other as enemy.

In his first return to Croatia since it had declared independence from the former Yugoslav state, Miroslav Volf experienced, as he describes it, a certain freedom finally to be himself in his homeland. This freedom, Volf explains, was short-lived. He soon sensed an unexpressed expectation to explain why as a Croat he still had friends in Serbia and did not talk with disgust about the backwardness of their culture. "The new Croatia, like some jealous goddess, wanted all my love and loyalty," says Volf.

In labeling another as enemy, we are not likely to see him or her as being like us. The thought of my being in any way like my opponent is distasteful. After all, *I* am just being flexible. *She* is unreliable. *We* are prudent. *They* are obstructing progress. *We* are good. *They* are evil. Perception is a powerful force in conflict. How I see things depends on where I am standing, what glasses I am looking through. At my worst, I may see the same behavior that is so detestable in them as virtuous in me.

One way of nurturing people through even the most difficult of conflicts is to help them to see ways in which they are like their opponents and vice-versa. The challenge, so difficult in conflict, is to get each to see the basic humanity of the other, complete with the wounds that are a part of the past. We see the challenge in the story of Cain and Abel:

> In the course of time Cain brought to the Lord an offering of the fruit of the ground, and Abel for his part brought of the firstlings of his flock, their fat portions. And the Lord had regard for Abel and his offering, but for Cain and his offering he had no regard. So Cain was very angry, and his countenance fell. The Lord said to Cain, "Why are you angry, and why has your countenance fallen? If you do well, will you not be accepted? And if you do not do well, sin is lurking at the door; its desire is for you, but you must master it." Cain said to his brother Abel, "Let us go out to the field." And when they were in the field, Cain rose up against his brother Abel, and killed him. Then the Lord said to Cain, "Where is your brother Abel?" He said, "I do not know; am I my brother's keeper?" And the Lord said, "What have you done? Listen; your brother's blood is crying out to me from the ground!" (Gen. 4:3-10)

Here rivalry between two brothers, filled with envy and fueled by anger, turns to hatred and murder. Cain's murderous act was deeply connected to something he later denies to the Lord—that his identity was, from the beginning, shaped in relation to his brother. Cain's solution to the conflict was to kill Abel. Afterward, out in the field, the Lord asked Cain, "Where is your brother Abel?" Cain replied, "I do not know; am I my brother's keeper?" By getting rid of Abel, Cain was trying to exclude him from his life for good.

Embracing the Other

A second way of dealing with differences is to embrace the other.

In the story of the Prodigal Son (Luke 15:11-32), the younger son who goes off to squander his inheritance makes every effort to break from the identity forged by his household. He finds himself yearning for the life that once defined his very being, even if that meant returning as one "no longer worthy to be called your son" (vv. 18, 21). Perhaps most amazing is that the father had never let go of his relationship with this son, had never abandoned his identity as a father to this lost one.

Angry, the older brother refuses to readjust an identity he had become accustomed to—that of faithful elder and only son. There was no longer any space in him for such a prodigal. Ultimately, he must reshape his identity in light of a new status quo based on a changed relationship. The younger son has returned, but the conflict and its transformation does not allow for a return to what once was. The younger son's breach, the older son's resistance, and the father's forgiving embrace have not left anyone unchanged.

At the heart of the cross, claims Miroslav Volf, are the open arms of Christ's self-giving love embracing us, the enemy. For "while we were enemies, we were reconciled to God through the death of his Son," wrote the apostle Paul (Rom. 5:10a). In the ultimate sacrifice, Christ created space in himself to receive estranged humanity. Despite demands made on Christians and non-Christians alike by nations and corporations, God's people are called to a radical embrace of those whom others would deem the "enemy" in human conflict (Matt. 5:43, 44). Those transformed in Christ are called to make space in themselves not only for friends but for enemies.

When issues at the core of our identity come into conflict, more is needed than the recognition that, as a human being, I am like my enemy. The other is not just like my self—but part of my self. I am not independent, but interdependent. If my opponent is eliminated, something of my self is lost. Lost as well is the possibility of repentance in the pursuit of justice, the hope of achieving reconciliation, the transformation of right social relationships, and the gift of undeserved forgiveness from God.

The Transforming Power of Conflict

Transforming Who We Are

Before my oldest son Seth had mastered some of the more difficult gymnastics of the English language, he would on occasion create some interesting forms of speech. Once when trying to test whether I was telling the truth about something, he asked, "Papa, are you true?" At first I was tempted to correct him, but after thinking for a moment I was struck by the insight that his mistake had provided. If I am a person committed to telling the truth (Matt. 5:33-37), then I become a person of the truth. Or, in Seth's way of saying it, a true person.

Some of the more insightful discussions of character and virtue in the last few years have emphasized the close relationship between our identity and our actions. What we do is who we are or become. The husband caught up in an affair begins to structure his life around lies he must tell to conceal his secret. Soon his whole life becomes a lie. We have seen that who we are can be profoundly shaped by conflicts around us, for better or worse. Conflict has the ability to transform our perceptions of self and others, our relationships, our whole social setting.[8] Conflict is a powerful agent of change, able even to transform our identities.

Transforming What We Do

In the sermon he preached at his father's funeral, Stanley Hauerwas reflected on his father's lifelong gentleness. That his father's gentleness "was so effortless," he wrote, "helps us better understand Jesus' Beatitudes."[9] They are not, as we typically think of them, ideals we must strive to attain. Rather, those who answer the call to follow Jesus will find themselves becoming meeker, or poorer in spirit, and better peacemakers. Who we are as Christians will transform what we do.

Nowhere is this more important than in conflict. In his book on Christian civility, Fuller Seminary president Richard J. Mouw lists traits for living as God's people in an uncivil world.[10] Mouw encourages us to be *flexible* rather than rely on neat formulas. We are to be *tentative* in letting ideological commitments of "right" or "left" define us or God. Mouw admonishes us to approach God and others with *humility*, acknowledging that no one can grasp all of God's revealed truth (Rom. 11:33-34). We are to be filled with *awe* at God's unending mercy and grace toward us and called to find our place in God's larger project with a sense of *modesty* about how each person fits into the body of Christ.

Conclusion

This is what transforming ourselves in conflict is all about: *treating others in ways that are consistent with who God calls us to be as God's people.* God works through conflict to transform us so that we might in turn transform the pain and injury of conflict into opportunities for healing, forgiveness, and reconciliation. That is the work God calls us to do. That is the kind of people God calls us to become.

Discussion Questions

1. Mention a conflict that has changed the people involved. Is the change for better or worse?

2. Which force do you think of as stronger: conflict changing who we are—or who we are in changing conflict? Why?

3. Try to identify an individual or group with no obvious influence

on who you are. Search for ways you may be affected by that person or group. Ask others for some help with this.

4. Have you ever made space in you for an "enemy" by embracing that person? How did it affect you?

5. Are there things about who you are that you feel could never change? What are they? Would you be willing to negotiate those things with someone else? Why or why not?

6. How does conflict change what you do? Do you respond as well as you would like? Why or why not? What would you change if you could?

3

Cultural Dynamics and Conflict

By Regina Shands Stoltzfus

Regina Shands Stoltzfus lives in Cleveland, Ohio, with her husband, Art, and their four children. She is associate pastor at Lee Heights Community Church, a racially mixed congregation she has attended since childhood. She is also co-coordinator of Damascus Road, an Anabaptist antiracism education and organizing process. Her interest in conflict transformation comes from a deep belief that the message of reconciliation is at the core of the gospel, and that Jesus came to heal and to invite us to be healers. She wants her work in the world to be part of that healing of fractured relationships and fractured people.

The Sleepover

Not long ago my daughter had her first sleepover. Over the course of the evening, the five six-year-old girls ate pizza and sundaes, played dress-up and other imaginary games, watched a video, and tried to escape the advances of my two-year-old son. It was a fun time, but the later it got, the more tired and grumpy the girls became. As I ushered them upstairs to bed, the final argument of the evening was over which girl would sleep where. Rachel's bed was big enough for two girls, so three would have to sleep on the floor in sleeping bags. They couldn't agree on what was fair.

Finally one girl proposed a solution. "I have an idea," Marita said. "All the black people should sleep on the bed, and the white people should sleep on the floor."

The numbers worked out—there were two African-American girls, including my daughter. The others, including Marita, were white. I asked her why she thought that was a good solution.

She replied, "Well, in the old days, the black people got all the

47

bad stuff, and the white people got all the good stuff. So the black people should get good stuff now."

We worked out the sleeping arrangements without using race as the deciding factor, but I was fascinated by Marita's proposal and the thought she had put into it. As young as she was, she knew people's cultural backgrounds can and often do impact the way the world works for them—influencing how decisions are made, how resources are divided, and who goes where and with whom.

What Is Culture?

Culture has been described as "what everyone knows that everyone else knows" in a group. I am a first-generation Northerner. During the Great Migration of the 1940s and '50s, thousands of African-Americans left the rural South for the urban centers of the North—Chicago, Cleveland, New York, and others—seeking employment and an escape from segregation and discrimination.

When I was a child, every summer we traveled to the South to visit relatives. My southern cousins were shocked at my rudeness when I didn't say "Yes, ma'am" or "No, sir" on addressing adults. I was surprised at their formality, but I made the adjustment. Down there, everyone knew you were supposed to address adults in that formal manner. It was a cultural value of the South, and a cultural norm. My ignorance of that norm caused people I cared about to think I was rude, which I like to think I was not. To change this *perception*, I had to change my *behavior* and adjust to that which the culture—what everyone knew—dictated.

Groups, each with their own culture, unconsciously and consciously influence how people interact with each other. In addition to race, Rachel's group of sleepover pals represented several other kinds of groupings. They all belonged to the gender group we call girls. Four were from Christian families, one was Jewish. Three of the girls attended the same elementary school and were in the same first grade class. They all lived in racially mixed cities.

Groupings affect all of us, not just six-year-old girls. For people of color, racial identification becomes a particularly strong source of pride and point of allegiance. The desire to connect with others who share this identification is a driving force behind the push for multicultural education. Gender is another grouping with a major influence on interactions. Men interact differently with other men than with women. Women act differently with other women than with men.

Sometimes we put ourselves in groups. Sometimes others put us in groups. Race and gender are frequently groups into which people can be placed without even talking because of visible characteristics. If anything, we become more self-defining in the context of cultural groupings as we become older.

Culture and Power

There is an exercise used in diversity training known as "Ups and Downs." It is usually done toward the beginning of the training to help people see the amount of diversity in the room and also to let people self-identify the groups to which they belong. The facilitator asks people to stand up when a particular group they belong to is called out—"If you speak a language other than English, stand up. If you live in a city, stand up. If you're a male, stand up. If you're middle-class, stand up."

The interesting thing about this exercise is that in many of the categories the people standing have an inverse power relationship with those left sitting. In North American society, men have more power than women. People with college degrees have more power than those without formal education. Middle-class people have more power than poor people. White people have more power than people of color.

When Cultures Clash

It seems impossible to pick up a newspaper and not read several accounts of incidents that stem from cross-cultural conflict. There are, of course, the blatant examples—schoolyard fights that begin with the hurling of racial epithets; acts of violence against women, gays and lesbians; and clashes between groups of differing religious beliefs. Then there are issues that seem more subtle in terms of the role culture plays—disputes over hiring and job dismissals, arguments about what curricula should be taught in public schools, and debates about "national language" and immigration policies.

Our churches are not immune to these struggles. What style of worship defines a congregation—quiet and predictable and fairly low-key, or spontaneous and lively, even loud? What kind of music—traditional hymns sung a capella, contemporary praise with a band, or down-home gospel with an organ and piano? Who shall lead? What do we believe about women in ministry? Can an African-American, Hispanic, Asian American, or Native American serve as senior pastor in a predominantly white congregation? Should liturgical dance be included in a worship service?

On an even deeper level, where does our church budget go? Whom do we invite in and of whom do we speak when we talk about "our" congregation? "Our" denomination? Whose faces are reflected in artistic representations of Jesus, of angels, of other biblical persons? How are these decisions made?

In considering these questions, we can see how the earlier discussion of power influences the outcome of discussions concerning being a community, a nation, the church. It is not only a matter of who is at the table for these discussions and the actions that follow but how much influence and power these folks have and how willing people are to step outside their comfort zone.

Culture is what we know, who we know, and how we do things. Cultural identities tell us who we are and give us a sense of belonging. However, we live in a world of various cultures and even cultures in cultures. We will bump up against each other and rub each other the wrong way from time to time.

A temptation, particularly in the church, is to segregate ourselves from one another—or at least to deny our differences and focus on areas we have in common. This kind of thinking hampers our growth, both as individuals and communities. We are not free to be the persons and communities God created us to be if we deny our diversity and don't fully use the gifts we all bring.

God's People Coming Together

Because churches are not buildings but people, they are constantly shifting and changing. Though Christ, the foundation, remains the same from generation to generation, the church makes adjustments to reflect the times and the people of the moment. We are currently undergoing one of those shifts as congregations recognize the need to live out the inclusive message of the gospel and become places where there truly is "no male or female, no Jew or Greek."

But those changes do not come easily. Our approaches to cultural diversity and inclusiveness in the church have tended to be all or nothing propositions. Either we seek to melt differences into a tasteless stew (or one that tastes only of the dominant culture), or we segregate ourselves. In addition, institutions by their very nature tend to resist change. Institutions are in the business of staying the same. That's what we mean when we say an idea or a project has become "institutionalized"; it has become an immovable, unchangeable part of the whole.

This idea of changing the face of the church is not new. In fact, it has been grappled with since the church's infancy. One such accounting is in the tenth chapter of Acts (10-12).

Peter and Cornelius

In this chapter, Cornelius has a vision of an angel, and Peter has a most wondrous dream about food. Tired and hungry, Peter ascends a rooftop to pray.

> And he became hungry, and was desiring to eat, but while they were making preparations, he fell into a trance; and he beheld the sky opened up, and a certain object like a great sheet coming down, lowered by four corners to the ground, and there were in it all kinds of four-footed animals of the earth and birds of the air. (NASB)

"Eat, Peter," a voice urges. "Eat." But Peter is a good Jewish boy, a follower of God's law as he understands it, and recognizes some of the food as unclean—food he must not eat. "By no means, Lord, for I have never eaten anything unholy and unclean." The reply? "What God has cleansed, no longer consider unholy."

This is an entirely new concept for Peter. Things are not as he has supposed. The laws handed down from generation to generation have suddenly and radically changed. Although Peter is perplexed at first as to the meaning of this vision, things in time become clear. The Spirit speaks to Peter and tells of three men who are looking for him and says to go to them without misgivings. They are the men sent by Cornelius, who has been seeking God's face.

The lesson for Peter, of course, is that the Jesus he is preaching is not just for the Jews—the people like him. God was bigger than Peter had ever imagined, and God's family included those the Jews had deemed "unclean." "And all the circumcised believers who had come with Peter were amazed, because the gift of the Holy Spirit had been poured out on the Gentiles also" (Acts 10:45, NASB).

All these many years later, we still hold ideas about who is clean (us) and who is unclean (them), often based on cultural background. We still struggle with what it means to be the whole family of God amid diversity. Yet diversity is God's gift to us.

Crossing Boundaries

The accounting of the creation in Genesis is a litany of the world's diversity and God's proclamation of it all being "good." Evening and morning. Water and land. Plants bearing seed and trees bearing fruit; sun, moon and stars; all manner of living creatures that move in the sea, on the land and in the air. Male and female made in the very image of God.

How do we, in the center of all that makes us wonderfully different, come together in ways that further the church's mission and give each of us a place in it? How can we work through conflicts that arise between peoples who are different from one another? Here are places to begin.

Create Safe Spaces

We need to create safe spaces for each other to talk honestly about who we are, our hopes and fears. Much of our knowledge about the "other" is based on assumptions, stereotypes, and baggage from past hurts. Breaking through myths about each other can only happen through sitting together at the same table.

Have No Other Gods

We must refuse to idolize maleness, whiteness, wealth, and other worldly interpretations of who is powerful, who is "right" while others are "wrong." We need to recognize racism, sexism, classism, among other "isms." Upon recognizing and naming them, we need to begin to dismantle them.

Move beyond Good Intentions

We must recognize good intentions are not enough. Peter was already on fire for Christ and the building of the church, but he still thought the Gentiles were unclean. It took a radical intrusion of God's Spirit into Peter's life to send him places he never dreamed he would go.

Conclusion

Conflict is the result of differences that produce tension. It reflects our individual preferences, values, and lifestyles. It also connects with group preferences, values, and ways of doing things. Conflict transformation requires more than the commitment of individuals to seek peace with each other. It requires groups who respect other groups and are willing to adjust their rules, patterns, and organizations to make space for others. Lasting peace cannot be achieved without the transformation of the culture that surrounds us.

Discussion Questions

1. In your private life, who are "us" and "them?" In your congregational life? What are the boundaries? What are areas for growth?

2. Culture provides us with a design for living. What are obvious

ways culture affects the way you live? What are subtle ways it influences you?

3. Our culture can be invisible to us. How does this happen? How can we become aware of the way culture affects us? Is it possible to change culture?

4. Discuss a conflict that you believe has roots in cultural differences. Do you believe the conflict can be successfully transformed? Why or why not?

5. Who makes the decisions in your congregation? In what ways are these people alike? Different? Do you believe these likenesses or differences affect how decisions are made?

6. Do you think the story of Peter's dream and the decisions he made afterward has a message for the church today? For your congregation? For you as an individual?

COMMUNICATION AND CONFLICT TRANSFORMATION

EVERYONE COMMUNICATES. We can't help it. Even if we don't listen when a friend talks, we send a message: We communicate that we don't care enough—or are too preoccupied—to hear. Communication is an all-pervasive part of being human and at one level seems simple. James 1.19 gives this practical advice about communication: "Let everyone be quick to listen, slow to speak, slow to anger." But if it's so simple, why talk about it?

We talk about communication because it is so basic. Conflict transformation requires constructive communication. The more difficult the conflict, the more critical constructive communication is. Unfortunately, many of us do not communicate as well as we could. When our souls are tense, our speech often becomes muddled and our hearing becomes impaired. We can feel misunderstood or not heard at all. We can get angry. The tension can increase. With good communication, we connect with others. Effective communication alone does not transform conflict, but it is necessary for transformation to occur.

The next three chapters address communication. Chapter 4 focuses on listening, an underrated part of the process. Chapter 5 explores speaking, a frequently abused but critical part of communication. Chapter 6 examines dialogue, the interaction of speaking and listening. These are the tools which we need to master before conflict can be transformed. The better we handle these tools, the more successful our peacemaking efforts will be.

4

Listening

by Kori Leaman-Miller

Kori is a homemaker and artist with a master's degree in communication, specializing in transformation. She helped start two Victim-Offender Reconciliation Programs in Colorado. Kori previously served four years with Mennonite Central Committee in El Salvador. Her experience of living in the midst of the civil war there sparked her interest in learning constructive ways to deal with conflict. She lives in Denver with her husband Larry and two young sons.

The Wise Monk and the Student

There is a famous story of an earnest student who travels a long distance to visit a wise monk. The student arrives seeking wisdom, his head filled with questions. The seeker becomes extremely frustrated when his teacher refuses to answer his queries.

Finally the monk says, "Pour me a cup of tea and I will tell you when to stop." The student dutifully pours the tea—and keeps pouring and pouring until the cup overflows and spills onto the floor. Exasperated, the student finally bursts out, "Can't you see the cup is full? It can't hold any more!"

The wise teacher replies, "And so it is with you. Your mind is full of too many things. Only when you are empty will there be room for more to come in."[11]

Types of Listening

Many types of listening are required throughout a day. We may "browse" radio news, shifting attention between morning routines and reporters. If a story demands attention, we listen intently. We also listen for information when getting directions or learning new skills.

When in conversation with another, we may listen just to pass the time, to maintain the relationship, or to catch up on personal news. We sometimes use a surfing approach to conversational listening, particularly in groups: We tune in for a few minutes at a time, flip the channel to another point of interest (whether internal or external), and tune in again to make sure we haven't missed anything.

Critical listening is called for when a friend wants feedback on an idea or a speech. We also use critical listening when we disagree with what someone has said. We marshal our arguments, awaiting opportunity for rebuttal.

We listen to ourselves. Our bodies communicate, if we heed them. When our stomachs rumble, we recognize we are ravenous. When we yawn, we remember we stayed up too late the night before. When our muscles ache, we know we aren't as young as we were.

Then there is that most incessant communicator—our internal voice. (If you stop to listen right now, the voice in your head may insist, "I'm not saying anything! Honest!") We also use inner dialogue to think analytically about a situation: Why am I upset about this?

Active Listening

Striving to Understand

There is yet another type of listening: active listening. The goal of active listening is understanding, not to win an argument but to learn what another is thinking and feeling. Seeking to understand others does not imply agreeing with all they say; instead, it conveys that we care enough to try to understand their experience. At its best, active listening can result in a new understanding for the speaker as well. A good listener can help us discover a truth about ourselves that was previously obscure.

The single Chinese character for the verb *to listen* includes symbols for ears, eyes, undivided attention, and heart.[12] These symbols give clues about how to do this difficult skill. We hear the words with our ears. We attend to the speaker with our eyes. We focus our attention on their message. We understand and empathize with our hearts.

Working Together

Active listening is an interactive, face-to-face process that involves checking in with the speaker to discover if the meaning you have attached to the words is the same as the intended meaning. Active listening takes place when people listen to understand the other.

Listening to TV news may qualify as a search for understanding, but it is not interactive. (Yelling at the TV doesn't count.) Likewise, listening in conflict or conversation may be interactive but not necessarily a search for understanding. We may listen only long enough to confirm in our own minds that the other is dead wrong.

Active Listening and Conflict

Active listening can be used in many situations—from information gathering to supporting a friend, child, or loved one through a difficult hour or decision. Asking questions to make sure we understand directions is active listening. Asking a friend if you heard them correctly is active listening. Therapists are trained in active listening and use it often.

Active listening is useful for exploring and resolving conflict, whether as participant in conflict or as mediator. This type of listening allows the issues underlying a conflict to percolate to consciousness to be dealt with rather than remain boiling below the surface. Though difficult, active listening can be transformative. One critical part of active listening is that it must be perceived as genuine interest and not as technique.

The Power of the "Listened Word"

To actively listen we must create space in the cluttered corridors of our minds for communication to happen. When our cups are full—minds overflowing with our own affairs—we have no room for the concerns of another. The meaning of the words cannot enter; we cannot listen. When we choose actively to listen, to make space for another, we exercise a power that can have startling, life-giving effects.

Listening Another into Existence

"I'd like a hamburger and a glass of milk," the six-year-old said to the waitress.

"He'll have the child's portion of Salisbury steak with mixed vegetables," the mother said, ignoring the boy and ordering for him.

"And what would you like on your hamburger?" the waitress asked the boy.

Surprised, the boy looked up at her with puzzled, then brightening, eyes. "Just ketchup," he said.

After she left the table, the boy turned to his mother. "You know what?" he said. "She thinks I'm real."[13]

Mary Rose O'Reilley calls what the waitress did for the boy an act of "listening someone into existence."[14] Children and older people are often the victims of "nonlistening," but we all know how it feels. We launch into a story only to realize partway through that no one is listening. It's like we're not even there.

Active listening can transform a person from being "not there" to being present for us. Choosing actively to listen to someone is choosing to make them real in that moment. Active listening is in and of itself a gift, an affirmation of the speaker. Active listening transforms conflicts. Ears solve more clashes than words do.

The Power of Being Heard

Several years ago I helped discussions between longtime members of a parish who were in conflict with a relatively new resource person. During the course of the sometimes heated debate, one man spoke with feeling about respect for religious tradition. As I listened, it occurred to me that his faith was crucial to him. When I said as much, I could almost hear a "thwack" as I hit the bull's-eye of their conflict over worship styles: respect for differing approaches to faith, including the traditional approach. The man sat down and said not another word, satisfied that his meaning had been heard. That "listened word" was a turning point in the discussions, resulting in more openness on all sides.

Getting Beneath the Things That Matter

When my husband and I were co-directors of Mennonite Central Committee's program in war-torn El Salvador, we once sat down with a couple who were having a tough time finishing their assignment in a very conflicted part of the country. They questioned whether they should leave their assignment several months early. I entered the conversation thinking that they wanted to leave. Assuming they struggled with guilt feelings, I decided I would try to make it easier for them to go. Boy, was I off the mark.

They wanted to finish their term in El Salvador. This was why they had asked for the meeting—to work at ways to make staying possible. Based on my preconceived idea that they were ready to go home, I didn't hear what they were saying. I made remarks that made them feel like I was trying to push them out the door. I hurt their feelings because I did not use that conversation as a process for discovering truth.

A former instructor of mine pictured conflict—or, indeed, conversation—as an iceberg. Only a tiny percentage of a dilemma or feeling is visible at the start. Active listening helps expose the vast chunk of interests and emotions that are hidden from view. In this mass of "hidden agenda" we can find the basis for understanding and, ultimately, resolution.

Listening to God

When we pray, how often do we say: "Speak, Lord, for your servant is listening?" More often, I think, we say: "Listen, Lord, for your servant is speaking!"[15]

Many spiritual authors, from our desert fathers and mothers to Anthony de Mello and Sue Monk Kidd, have written about the importance of silence—of listening—in prayer. Even in communication with God, the words of James apply, "Be quick to listen, slow to speak, slow to anger" (1:19).

De Mello says that we cannot learn to know God because we think we already do.[16] He says our preconceived ideas of God are, in fact, barriers to growth in prayer. To leap this obstacle, we must come to God, not with lists of needs and wants, but in silence. Only through the "listened word" can we transform our spiritual lives.[17]

Why Is Listening Hard to Do?

Active listening is easier to write about than do. Active listening is not feasible or appropriate all the time, but sometimes we can't do it even when we want to. What gets in the way?

Internal Noise

One day my three-year-old son came into the bathroom as I was blowing my hair dry. Because of the dryer noise, a minute passed before I realized he was talking to me. The prattle in our "head world" is sometimes like that hair dryer. Our "self-talk" is so loud we can't hear anything else. Our internal dialogue—about a previous conversation or a task that needs to be done or what we are going to say as soon as we get the chance—may be more compelling to us than the words waltzing from another's mouth.

One reason it's hard to control this inside-the-brain chatter is physiology. We are capable of understanding up to 600 words per minute, but the average person says less than 140 words per minute.[18] Our minds are left with time for wandering.

Preconceived Ideas

Part of our internal talk is the experiences, prejudices, and assumptions that make us who we are. De Mello's insight about the barrier formed by preconceived ideas of God applies to our union with people as well. We often enter conversation with assumptions of what the other will think, feel, and say. This is true especially if the speaker is someone we have known for a long time. We face someone "different" than us with prejudices or stereotypes that cloud our ability to listen.

External Noise

In addition to all the yammering going on *inside* our heads, we are besieged with noise from radios, TVs, household appliances, traffic, other people—the list goes on. A former professor of mine who works at helping early heart attack victims reduce tension claims that noise is the number one stressor in our lives. Even soothing music is irritating to me when the general noise level in our house gets too high.

Motivation

Though we are bombarded with noise from inside and out, almost all of us can use active listening when it matters. All we need is the motivation. Think about dating. When conversing with someone we're attracted to, we can listen carefully while he or she recites the phone book. Or when trying to follow directions to a place we really want to get to, we ask focused questions.

We do know how to listen actively when it suits our purposes. The problem is that often we're too tired, hungry, busy, stressed, or otherwise mentally occupied to listen well.

What Must We Do to Hear?

Listening is *not* a natural ability. It is something we learn and relearn all of our lives. So how do we do it?

Create the Space

Active listening is an exclusive activity. We can't do it well with minds absorbed in cooking supper, listening to the radio, or chewing on a problem of our own (although a leisurely walk may work). When we choose active listening, we must mentally create the space for another's feelings, thoughts, and problems to enter consciousness. We need to stop what we are doing, turn off the radio, focus on the other person.

When distracting thoughts re-enter our minds—as they will—we need to notice them, then let them go. As we practice active listening and staying in the moment, suddenly we begin to hear not only what people are saying but what they are *trying* to say. Listening "seeks to both hear the words and hear beyond them to understand deeply the essence of their message. It means setting aside, for the moment, my agenda, my opinions, my feelings and focusing, with all my capability, on the other and what is important to them."[19]

There are times, however, when our own problems are so consuming we find it impossible to abandon our own agenda. We simply cannot listen—we cannot create the space. This is important to recognize. We do others a favor if we tell them honestly that we are unable at the moment to be good listeners.

One way to create space for listening is to do nothing—to wait. Waiting is tough for many of us from cultures that love words. However, if we are willing to try it, we will find that waiting in silence can apply its own gentle pressure to the other person. Asking an open-ended question and then simply waiting for a response—though the silence grows uncomfortably long—can provide just the space needed for a new insight to appear. You may find that the other person will "check in" with her eyes, to make sure you are really there, listening. Stay with it. It is often just after that visual "check-in" that disclosure comes.

Paraphrase

Years ago I took part in a training on conflict resolution. The instructor was describing the use of paraphrasing when a woman stood up and said, "I can't stand it when someone repeats what I've just said. It makes me feel like a child." The instructor responded, "You mean when someone parrots what you've just told them, you feel like you aren't being taken seriously?" The woman responded emphatically, "Yes, exactly!" The group erupted into laughter as she sat down, convinced that she'd been heard and understood because of the instructor's skillful paraphrasing.

This story illustrates two points about paraphrasing: When done well, it is highly effective. But, as the woman pointed out, sometimes paraphrasing feels fake or even offensive if it comes across as a technique rather than genuine interest.

Active listening is not about saying nothing. Once we create a space in our minds for communication to happen, other skills are helpful. Paraphrasing is a response that lets speakers know you are with them. Paraphrasing simply means to put the speaker's thoughts into your own words, to make sure you understand them.

Ask Questions

There are hundreds of thousands of words in the English language, though most of us use about 2000. The 500 most common words have 14,000 dictionary definitions.[20] As if that were not enough, the inflection that we give to a word can change the meaning of a sentence. Given all the variables, how do we know we have received the message that the speaker intended to send?

The obvious answer is to ask questions. It seems almost simplistic to include "asking questions" in this chapter, yet this is a technique we don't use as often as we could. We assume we understand what someone else means yet often find ourselves misunderstood.

Asking questions is an excellent way to increase our understanding and to indicate our interest in the other person. We can ask questions to clarify, to help another define a problem more precisely, or to encourage someone to delve more deeply into an issue: "How did you feel when they turned you down?"

Questions can be used inappropriately as well. Sometimes we ask questions which satisfy our curiosity but only prove distracting to the speaker. Other times we may criticize or make suggestions disguised as questions: "Are you sure that was the best thing to do?" This type of questioning lets the speaker know you've got a pretty good idea of how to solve their problem. It's a good way to slam the door on discovery.

Make Sure Your Body Agrees with Your Words

All the silence, paraphrasing, and questioning in the world will not communicate an active listening attitude if your body delivers a different message. Nods, eye contact, physically facing a person, coming to the same level (sitting if the other is sitting, stooping to the level of a child) are ways of creating space for communication to happen. If our nonverbal language disagrees with our words, our bodies are more believable than what we say. When we are really engaged with someone, our body posture will often unconsciously mimic that person's posture. It is important to remember that what is comfortable and appropriate in terms of body language will vary somewhat from culture to culture.

Conclusion

Douglas Steere wrote, "To 'listen' another's soul into a condition of disclosure and discovery may be almost the greatest service that any human being ever performs for another."[21] Listening is the work of a lifetime. When we empty our cups to listen to another, we give the other and ourselves a gift: we experience that mysterious moment that has the power to transform relationships.

Discussion Questions

1. Think of the person who is your best listener. What characteristics make that person stand out in your mind?

2. Do you find active listening, as described in this chapter, difficult or easy to do? What things do you do well? What gets in the way of "creating the space to listen"? Which of these things can you change? How?

3. Think of a conflict you have had. List the assumptions you made about the conflict or about the other person(s). How did your assumptions affect your ability to listen? If the conflict has not yet been resolved, how could active listening affect the outcome?

4. Have you experienced being "listened into existence"? Have you ever offered this gift to another? What happened? Are particular people or groups of people ignored more than others? Why is listening empowering?

5. Why is authenticity essential to active listening? What happens when we use the techniques without genuine interest in the response?

6. Evaluate your prayer life. How much time do you spend in speaking and how much in listening? How do you go about listening in prayer?

5

Speaking

by Valerie Weaver-Zercher

Valerie Weaver-Zercher was employed most recently as assistant director of the Lancaster (Pa.) Mediation Center and as teacher of English-as-a-Second-Language. From 1996-1998 she was assistant and managing editor of Gospel Herald, the news and theology magazine of the Mennonite Church. Currently she works on freelance writing and editing projects and is contemplating graduate school. She lives in Harrisburg, Pa., with her husband Dave, with whom she has conflict on a regular basis and with whom she is learning (slowly) to speak her mind and her heart.

Longing to Speak

The orchard row stretching down the slope to my right dangles with ripe apples. I'm standing on a cart pushed into the branches of one of these trees, nudging crimson globes from stems and laying each carefully in a wooden crate at my feet. Every so often I glance up at the orchards and vineyards running out in every direction, field after emerald field pushing up against the ridge of distant mountains.

As I work, I'm enveloped by the chatter of German women, workers my host family hires every fall to help out with the harvest. They're round, ruddy, comfortable women, with laugh lines and slight limps—not that different from my aunts in Pennsylvania, I think. But they speak only German, and I, a month into an exchange program, speak barely any. They ask me questions and tell me little stories, giggling sympathetically when I can't understand and sometimes petting my arm as if I'm a cute puppy. Sometimes they almost yell in my ear, hoping with that universal hope that if they speak louder, I might comprehend their words.

I smile weakly and swallow and blink to keep the tears from coming. I want to speak, to tell them about my life in the United

States, to tell them little jokes and stories, to tell them that they remind me of my aunts. Here I am, in probably the most beautiful valley in the world, I think, and I am utterly miserable. It is because I cannot speak.

The Gift of Speech

We are often unaware of the gift of speech until it is taken from us. Loss of voice—whether due to a cross-cultural experience, psychic, social, or political marginalization, or even just laryngitis—can be frightening and even damaging. As I experienced at the beginning of my year in Germany, loss of language is often accompanied by loss of security and sense of self. Speech enables us not only to communicate with others but also to communicate with ourselves. Indeed, we are often able to make sense of certain ideas, emotions, or events only after we have begun trying to explain them to another.

Speaking can be dangerous, just as listening can; it can force us to confront realities we'd rather avoid. It can do intended or unintended damage to others. We use speech to hurt and to heal, to express and to avoid expressing feelings, to convince others and to convince ourselves, to fight and to avoid fighting, to assert and to belittle ourselves.

Why is loss of speech so paralyzing and its use so dangerous? Speech holds an almost supernatural power; indeed, if the first words spoken (according to Genesis 1) are any indication, we'd do well to reexamine the reaches of its power. With one short speech, "Let there be light," God created light and darkness and day and night, which became the stage for the rest of the creation drama. Simple words, simply stated, had the power to bring into being seas and land, sun and moon, creatures in water and land and sky, even human beings. God spoke; things happened. Creation was as simple—and as complicated—as speech.

Though we obviously can't bring forth swarms of living creatures, we do have the power to create and destroy through speech that parallels God's own. Being aware of this power is the first step toward learning to speak with both the truth in our minds and the compassion in our hearts, especially in conflict. Indeed, speaking in conflict holds special power to destroy and to uplift. To move a conflict beyond stagnation and toward transformation, we must be willing to speak both what is on our mind and in our hearts. But before we examine specific ways of speaking in conflict, let's look at a few reasons people speak and remain silent. Why are some people paralyzed by the thought of speech? Why do others speak too much?

Why Don't I Speak
More Often and More Forcefully?

I Don't Know How I Feel

People sometimes remain silent, especially in a conflict, because they can't identify the emotions frothing inside. Rather than risk saying something they'll regret or don't mean, they say little or nothing. This silence can be interpreted as apathy, anger, or strategic disengagement by other parties. Such perceptions can lead to misunderstandings and further conflict.

I Want You to Know What I'm Thinking

Sometimes people remain silent in a conflict, especially with a significant other, because they think the other should be able to guess what they're thinking and feeling. Many of us have been hoodwinked by the myth of magic intimacy: if you really love me, you should know what I'm feeling without my having to *say* it. Such mind reading is not only impossible but also undesirable. If I want you to know what is going on inside of me, I must tell you. It is by the very act of my telling—and your listening—that this elusive and holy thing called intimacy is brought into being.

I Have Not Been Allowed to Speak in the Past

A history of not being heard, whether as a person or member of a group, is hardly the best encouragement to try speaking now. Sometimes people don't speak because layers of oppression and a history of violence prevent speech. Such power imbalances not only disable people from speaking their minds and hearts; they cheat the whole group out of those persons' ideas and perspectives. It's important to attend to reasons one woman in a roomful of men isn't speaking or the lone African American among whites remains silent.

Why Do I Speak
Too Often and Too Forcefully?

I Don't Know How I Feel

If I am unaware of my emotions and unable to name them, I may become forceful and even oppressive instead of remaining silent. Distance from my emotional center may make me insensitive to others' emotions as well. This in turn may make me railroad my ideas past others without listening to theirs. Insecurity is commonly and often rightly considered a reason to remain silent—but it can also lead to forceful expressions of opinions and domineering conversational techniques. Often when someone is oppressive or even lashing out, that aggression is emerging, consciously or unconsciously, from a deeper pain, woundedness, or self-doubt.

I Want You to Know What I Am Thinking

Much of the speech in the media and public arena these days is contentious and divisive. Growing up in this society, children learn that the goal in any argument is to win. By extension, the goal in any conversation is to convince. If I speak too often and too forcefully, chances are that I am operating in this paradigm that honors the debater and belittles (or at least ignores) the collaborator.

In our increasingly litigious culture, we are taught to present evidence, to prove something happened or didn't happen, and to "make a case." In other words, we learn to document, defend, and declare. All of this makes it easier for many of us to let others know what we are thinking than to listen to what they have to say.

I Have Always Been Allowed to Speak

If I am a member of a group with a history of dominance or that currently wields much power, I may be accustomed to speaking freely and to having the upper hand in conversations. I may come across as overbearing without knowing it. Recognizing my own power and learning to give others time and space to speak rather than filling every second with my own words is crucial.

How Then Should I Speak?

Interrogated

In her book *Vultures and Butterflies*, Susan Classen writes of her encounter with an interrogator from the Salvadoran military. Suspected of teaching Marxist doctrine due to her work with the poor, Classen was held for two days and repeatedly interrogated. "What is Marx's first name? Tell me everything you know about Marxism," her questioner prodded. "What do you teach in your Bible classes? Why do you talk about the poor working together? . . . Why do you teach the poor that God loves them?" While some of the questions stumped her, Classen didn't have to think long before she answered the last question. "I teach the poor that God loves them because it's true," she responded simply.[22]

Most of us won't undergo such an interrogation during our lifetimes. We can, however, learn much from the honest, clear, and unapologetic manner in which Classen spoke to the military officer. And while much less than our lives or freedom is at stake in our everyday conversations, our speech can still mirror the conviction and clarity with which Classen spoke. Indeed, speaking with integrity means speaking for myself, speaking clearly and simply, speaking when it is time, and speaking without apology.

For Myself

It's tempting to call on the chorus of others in a conflict. I can't count the times that, during my work at a community mediation center, I've heard, "*Everybody* on the block agrees with me; these people have to leave," and "I'm not the only one who feels this way; *everyone* has trouble with her." Whether as a mediator or a person in conflict, it's my job both to speak for myself and to encourage others to do the same.

"I-messages" are one way to speak for myself. The ubiquitous I-message has become worn and often formulaic. Nevertheless, the principles on which it is built are critical in communicating effectively, especially in conflict. The form can look something like this: "*I feel* [state the feeling] *when you* [state the behavior] *because* [state the effect]."

The goal of an I-message is to communicate to another one's feelings and reactions in a way that allows the other to remain nondefensive. I-messages are the inverse of blaming statements, which focus only on the other person's behavior and usually just end up making her or him defensive. Just as paraphrasing necessitates truly *listening to another*, I-messages require me to *listen to myself* and what I'm feeling at a given moment. Only then can I articulate what I'm feeling to the other in a way that frees the other to consider solutions to our *common* dilemma rather than immediately to defend her/himself.

It's easy to mistake the first piece of the message, "I feel," with a chance to tell persons what I *think* about them or the event. For example, "I feel that you are unfair and rude when you throw work at me and expect it to be done the next day," and "I feel that you turned my words around and misrepresented me when you told Julia what I told you in confidence" are not true I-messages. They might masquerade as such, since they both begin with "I feel," but they express judgment and opinions rather than emotions. I might as well say, "You are unfair and rude," and "You gossip! You intentionally misrepresented me."

How much more radical and difficult—not to mention uncomfortable—to discover what I really *feel* and admit it to the other person. How much more arduous—and rewarding—to say, "I feel frustrated when you give me work to do today that you want finished tomorrow because then I have to work late," and "I felt hurt and sad when you told Julia something that I wanted to be just between us. Now I'm afraid it will keep being passed around the office." Regardless of the exact form, authentic I-messages are always in some way self-revelatory; they admit to feelings that often hide under our surface anger or our carefully constructed public faces.

A common misconception about I-messages is that they're wimpy or emotionless. Who wants to work through conflict with someone so distant as to be able to state in a maddeningly flat voice, "I feel hurt when you . . ."? I-messages must emerge from an attitude of caring and a commitment to communicate. They should be spoken in a voice that matches the level of emotional intensity in the conflict.

Using I-messages is a hallmark of "centered speaking," as mediator Ron Kraybill defines it. "[Centered speaking] requires self-awareness . . . vulnerability . . . careful thought, and self-discipline," he writes. "Only those motivated by mature love are willing to invest the effort in this emotional and spiritual discipline that gets easier with practice."[23]

Clearly and Simply

Centered speaking also includes talking about specifics rather than general problems. When possible, it's helpful when others can know *exactly* what upset me last night and *which* words or concepts offended. Specificity decreases the other's defensiveness and moves the conflict forward rather than bogging it down in a morass of abstract generalities.

Simplicity is another hallmark of centered speaking. Avoiding jargon is usually a good idea; legalese, theology-speak, and any other "-ese" or "-speak" mostly annoys. When Jesus said, "Let your word be 'Yes, Yes' or 'No, No'; anything more than this comes from the evil one," (Matt. 5:37), he could have been talking about more than swearing. In conflict, it's usually better to err on the side of simplicity than complexity or confusion; too often, many words serve only to cloud the issues.

When It Is Time

I'm a Slow Thinker

Essayist and poet Kathleen Norris writes of an awkward encounter after she had given a lecture. "During the discussion period, one colleague, clearly frustrated with my response to a comment he'd made, said, 'Kathleen, you could have come back at me much harder on that.' He then proceeded to list several points I might have made, and I nodded my assent to most of them. Finally, I said, 'You know, Bill, I might have come up with all that, if I had more time, maybe two or three weeks. A month. I'm no good on my feet. I'm a slow thinker.' At least we all left that seminar wide awake. Uneasy, but awake."[24]

Speaking can require a lot of forethought, especially in certain situations and for certain individuals. It is not always possible—or even desirable—to speak immediately one's thoughts and feelings before mulling them over alone. Especially in conflict, people sometimes need space and time before they can express their emotions, needs, and ideas in a way that is both true to themselves and compassionate to the other person. Rather than yelling obscenities and insults, or becoming silent and withdrawn, it can help to agree to talk later when both parties can more clearly think about and feel what has happened. That's not to say that conflict should be rational or devoid of emotion; the point is to think and *feel* clearly. But time can often clarify both thoughts and feelings that are too jumbled to articulate while conflict is hot.

On the other hand, it's possible to think about a conflict *too long*, thereby letting it fester into something unmanageable. "Don't let the sun go down on your anger" is not a biblical injunction against experiencing emotions or getting rid of them as fast as possible; rather, it is a profound plea for direct communication and the forthright handling of disputes.

Even though explosive anger can be frightening and causes many people to attempt to hide their anger, authors Ruth Koch and Kenneth Haugk write of an equally frightening form of anger: that which *implodes* on itself as a result of not being expressed outwardly. "What people hide and deny will dominate them," they write.[25] Indeed, unspoken anger can evolve into depression, addiction, or physical sickness. As Koch and Haugk claim, denied emotions become dominating ones.

Of course the difficulty in speaking "when it is time" is figuring out when it's best to wait and when it's best to speak right now. Learning to listen to one's body, mind, and heart and being sensitive to the body, mind, and heart of the other is the best practice for determining when one needs to speak.

Without Apology

How many times have I expressed my feelings to someone and then apologized for them? Or perhaps even apologized for letting that person know how I felt? Probably more often than I'd like to admit. Speaking requires risk taking. One risk is that people will not like what I have to say. If I am truly speaking in a centered way with both truth and love, I do not need to apologize for expressing the way I feel, even if it brings undesirable reactions.

Theologian Elouise Renich Fraser writes, "When I speak in my own voice about troubling topics, I can count on tensions, unanticipated complications, misunderstandings, confusion, anxiety and distress, not just in my conversation partners but in me. I can also count on opportunities to consider other points of view and the possibility that with God's help we may find a better way."[26]

Where Technique Ends and Real Life Begins

This Stuff Won't Work Where I Come From

"You don't understand—this stuff won't work where I come from," one of the young men says during a seminar I am leading on I-messages and other communication skills. Voices around the room chime in in agreement. "Maybe if I were from some nice neighborhood where everyone talked like that, it'd work. But if I started talking that way in my neighborhood, I'm telling you, it wouldn't do any good. The only language people understand there is fists."

I stutter around, trying to defend these techniques while making clear my awareness that, as an upper-middle-class white woman, I don't know how tough it is to grow up on their streets. Inside I am kicking myself for even presuming to be able to teach them anything; these ideas are culturally foreign and probably inappropriate. I shouldn't have even agreed to lead this workshop, I think. Why should they listen to me?

Then a young man in the front row speaks up, turning slightly to his peers. "You don't have to use her words, like 'I feel this' and 'when' and 'because' and all that," he says. "But you can still let people know what effect they're having on you—especially people you really care about—by being honest about stuff and not acting all tough all the time." He proceeds to offer an honest, "untough," and self-possessed I-message—completely devoid of formula—for an example we had just been discussing.

A couple others nod their heads. We all sit in silence for a moment. I smile gratefully and a little meekly at the man in the front row. He and I and everyone else knows that his words have moved mountains mine never could.

Our speech is laden with all we have accumulated from our histories, families, churches, and neighborhoods. Recognizing that the very same words carry different and even opposite meanings for people of different cultures and backgrounds can move us toward an understanding of both the fragility and power of speech.

In the end, the impact of our words will depend more on our sincere desire to communicate than on the speaking techniques we employ. Indeed, a deep and abiding hunger for holy, compassionate, and inspired communication is the first and last step toward speaking for ourselves, listening to others, and ultimately speaking and listening to the Word that formed us.

Discussion Questions

1. Think about times you've felt unable to speak or express yourself. How did it feel to "lose your voice"? How did you recover it?

2. Do you tend to speak too little and too timidly or too often and too forcefully? What are reasons for the frequency and level of force with which you speak? What would it take for you to move, at least a little, toward the other end of the spectrum?

3. Reflect on times you've been on the receiving end of a You-message (the opposite of an I-message). How did you react to the blaming tone? When have you used accusatory, uncentered language? How did such conversation feel to you?

4. Reflect on attempts that you or others have made to use I-messages in conflict. Has the technique seemed awkward and unwieldy or natural and appropriate? Why?

5. Which is most difficult for you: To speak for yourself? To speak clearly and simply? To speak when it's time? To speak without apology? Think about encounters with others in which you did each of these well.

6. How can we express anger in a way that is both true to ourselves and not hurtful to others?

6

Transformation of Conflict Through Dialogue

Dalton Reimer

Though he grew up in a peace-loving family, Dalton acknowledges that conflict has not been absent from his life. Indeed, he remembers that when still a young child, he once attacked his brother with a hoe in a fit of rage. Each role he has subsequently played on the stage of life has added to his memory bank of conflict, including those of student, husband, parent, teacher, leader, and Co-Director of the Center for Peacemaking and Conflict Studies at Fresno Pacific University. Sometimes these conflicts have been handled constructively, sometimes destructively. Dalton says his theology of peacemaking has often been better than his practice. He has observed the same in others. Bringing his practice in line with his theology is one of his life goals.

Dialogue: From Existence to Friendship

In 1982 Simha Flapin, an elderly Jewish leader in the peace movement in Israel, shared a story with us at the Tantur Ecumenical Center near Jerusalem. He told us how frustrated he had become in earlier years of working for peace between Jews and Arabs in the Middle East. He and his colleagues would arrange meetings between Arabs and Jews. But when the Jews arrived, the Arabs would walk out.

Simha approached Martin Buber, the great Jewish thinker and advocate of dialogue, who was teaching in Jerusalem at the time. "How do you have dialogue if one side walks out when the other side shows up?" he asked Buber.

77

"To have dialogue doesn't require presence, only existence," replied Buber.

Initially Simha's story puzzled me. What did Buber mean? Then I remembered. Yes, that was what Buber had written.[27] Dialogue cannot happen without including the other. And including the other begins not with the other's presence, but with my recognition that the other truly exists.

About a decade after this gathering near Jerusalem, Israel's Prime Minister Yitzhak Rabin and Palestinian leader Yasser Arafat accepted an invitation to go to Washington, D.C., to make peace. In a dramatic televised climax to this meeting, Arafat and Rabin courageously reached out to each other and shook hands. It was a handshake felt around the world. *Time* chose these two—along with F. W. De Klerk and Nelson Mandela, former opponents in South Africa—as 1993 "men of the year." Lance Morrow, senior writer for *Time*, wrote, "It was against all the usual inclinations of the war devils that these four men took what must be the first step in the metaphysics of peace: they recognized the other's existence."[28]

Existence—the Beginning of Dialogue

Dialogue begins with existence—that is, with the recognition that all persons of whatever race, gender, class, or conviction are created in the image of God and are thus fully human. History is strewn with the wreckage of peoples whose existence others refused to recognize. Hence, this first step in dialogue has to do with me—with my own transformation. I must be willing to embrace the other as fully human and worthy of my attention and concern.

Jesus modeled this first step in dialogue. While we were still "sinners" and "enemies" of God (Rom. 5:8,10), Jesus came in human form to make peace between God and humankind and to establish a new kingdom of God. He was born into a specific family, tribe, and people in a specific place at a specific time. But unlike his contemporaries, he did not allow these specifics to bind him. Those others rejected he included. The kingdom he came to establish is inclusive. As Paul writes: "There is no longer Jew or Greek, there is no longer slave or free, there is no longer male and female; for all of you are one in Christ Jesus" (Gal. 3:28).

So in a specific conflict in a specific time and in a specific place, I am faced with these first questions: Does the other exist? Is the other fully human for me? If so, I will not demonize the other and so make the other seem less than human. Rather, I will meet the other as one who is as fully human as I am.

Friendship—The Highest Expression of Dialogue

Recognizing the other is the first step in dialogue. Other steps follow. For Buber, the highest expression of dialogue is found in friendship. So it is also with Jesus. When Jesus gave his farewell address to his disciples, he said, "I do not call you servants any longer, because the servant does not know what the master is doing; but I have called you friends, because I have made known to you everything that I have heard from my Father" (John 15:15).

Friendship, in these words of Jesus, is marked by a movement toward full disclosure—"I have made known to you everything that I have heard from my Father." Dialogue that leads to friendship is not withholding but disclosing. If information is power, dialogue is a process of power sharing. In sharing, Jesus moved from a position of domination to the side-by-side relationship of friends.

This leads to a second question when I am in conflict: am I prepared to disclose my thoughts and feelings and allow the other to disclose hers in a side-by-side relationship? If so, I will not seek to dominate the other but to disclose to her in a process of mutual truth seeking.

In Latin, the *com* of communication means "with." Dialogical communication is "withness" rather than "againstness." If I am willing to commit myself to disclosing and listening to the other's disclosures in the spirit of "withness," I leave the door open to friendship.

The "Spiritual Child" of Human Interaction

Loraine Halfen Zephyr suggests that in interacting with one another, we create between us a "spiritual child" no contraceptive can prevent. The space between us that was once void and empty is now filled. "If we come together in care, authenticity, honesty, and positive regard," Zephyr writes, "our child will be healthy, vibrant, winsome, and beautiful." When we come together through a mutual process of careful, sensitive listening and self-disclosing, we have dialogue. On the other hand, "if our child is created in dishonesty, exploitation, contempt, disregard, our child will be sickly, crippled, distorted, toxic, frustrated. It will be ugly."[29]

The Woman at the Well

On one of his journeys Jesus met a woman at a well rest stop in Samaria (John 4). She had come from the nearby village to draw water. With a simple request for a drink, Jesus dared enter the void between Jew and Samaritan. Recognizing the void, the woman responded, "How is it that you, a Jew, ask a drink of me, a woman of

Samaria?" From this tentative initial contact, their "spiritual child" began to fill the void between them as both listened and disclosed to the other at ever deeper levels. Through her subsequent witness, many others from her village meaningfully encountered Jesus, too.

We can expect, however, that dialogical initiatives will sometimes be resisted. Co-creating requires cooperation; not all are prepared to co-operate. Attempts to dialogue may be met with monological resistance. Our temptation in such situations may be to return kind for kind. "If you won't listen to me, I won't listen to you," we might be inclined to say.

Ruby Bridges

Ruby Bridges was six years old in 1960 when she began attending the traditionally all-white Frantz School in New Orleans. Her presence as an African-American was part of an effort to integrate the city's educational institutions. When she entered the first grade, all the white students boycotted the school in protest. Ruby faithfully attended school each day, though all alone. When she arrived each morning she would be greeted on the street by an angry mob of whites yelling obscenities at her and threatening to kill her. When she left in the afternoon the mob again surrounded her with their obscenities and threats. Federal marshals escorted her to and from school to protect her from the mob.

With the guidance and support of her family and church, Ruby chose not to return kind for kind. Instead, as she told child psychiatrist Robert Coles, she often prayed for the white mob on the street.

One morning, Ruby briefly paused in the midst of the mob on her way into school. Her teacher, watching through the window, saw her lips move. The teacher reported this to Coles. That evening, Coles met with Ruby in her home and asked her what she had said on the street. She said that she had been praying. When pressed further by Coles as to what she had said in her prayer, she replied, "Please, dear God, forgive them, because they don't know what they are doing."[30]

Creating a healthy "spiritual child" in our human interactions can be a challenge. Responding in kind to unloving behavior assures an unhealthy spiritual child. Responding with alternative behaviors increases the possibility that a sickly spiritual child may yet be restored to health. Biblical wisdom underscores this. Evil surprised by goodness is more likely to lead to a healthy spiritual child than evil met by evil (e.g., Prov. 15:1; 25:21-22; Matt. 5:38-48).

The Components of Dialogue

Listening

As mentioned in an earlier chapter, the Chinese character for listening combines the symbols for ears, eyes, and heart. Each symbol speaks to an important dimension of listening. Ears are for hearing. "Those who have ears to hear, let them hear," is a familiar biblical refrain. Hearing may be careless and superficial or careful and deep, as the refrain implies. Hearing, in the biblical sense, also moves one to action. To hear truth and not act on it is in the end not to hear. Eyes, though their appropriate use varies from culture to culture, communicate how we perceive a relationship and whether we are genuinely listening or not. Are we being attentive? Are we being respectful? Our eyes betray us. Whatever the cultural code, we communicate significantly with our eyes.

To listen with the heart is to listen with empathy for the other. When we listen with our hearts, we create the possibility of entering more deeply into the experience of the other. Dialogical listening unites ears, eyes, and heart in the enterprise of truly understanding the other.

Speaking

In speaking, the strong emotions of conflict easily lead to name-calling and accusatory, angry, and sometimes even dirty and profane words. While these may be designed to impress others with the intensity of our feeling, they may also offend and detract by becoming an issue in themselves. Expressing emotions and thoughts cleanly without resorting to offensive language helps keep the focus on the thoughts and feelings themselves, rather than on the way they are communicated.

When in conflict, simply and clearly identifying my concerns is of great value. It is not helpful to require the other to guess. Jesus said, "Let your word be 'Yes, Yes' or 'No, No'; anything more than this comes from the evil one" (Matt. 5:37). Clear and truthful speech reflects respect for both oneself and the other. Dialogical communication is neither giving in to nor dominating the other. Dialogical communication is bearing witness to the truth as I understand it, listening to the truth as the other understands it, and together seeking a common truth. Dialogical communication is truth speaking in a mutual process of truth seeking.

Head and Heart

"Speaking the truth in love" is the head and heart of dialogical communication (Eph. 4:15). Head without heart or heart without head is crippled communication. Wholeness requires both.

Different expressions have been used to capture the head and heart of dialogical communication. Jesus said, "be wise as serpents and harmless as doves" (Matt. 10:16, KJV). For Martin Luther King, these words of Jesus meant that one should be simultaneously "tough-minded" and "tender-hearted."[31] More recently, Richard Mouw has spoken of "convicted civility."[32] The expressions may change, but the essence is the same.

The Challenge of the Heart

Gandhi, the great leader of nonviolence during the twentieth century, observes in his autobiography that civility was the most difficult part of his movement. Civility, for Gandhi, did not "mean the mere outward gentleness of speech cultivated for the occasion, but an inborn gentleness and desire to do the opponent good."[33]

Whether we choose the language of civility or the biblical language of *agape* love, the challenge of the heart is the same. In contemporary usage *love* is unfortunately a mushy term, but in its biblical *agape* sense it is a strong, clear word. Its meaning is captured best in the teaching and modeling of Jesus and through the cluster of qualities identified by the apostle Paul (1 Cor. 13). These latter specific and concrete qualities are useful to review when in conflict. They can become a test of our readiness to engage the other.

The "L Scale" (Table 2, end of chapter) is an easy means of testing oneself in light of these qualities. If our score in a particular situation is low, perhaps our heart is not yet sufficiently prepared to engage the other. If our score is higher, we may be ready to proceed.

Face in Dialogue

Face concerns all of us. We have an image of ourselves. When something happens that detracts from this image, we can quickly become embarrassed and defensive. Indeed, if face becomes an issue in a conflict, we tend to give it priority over all other issues. That is why attention to face is so important in dealing with conflict.

Thrown into the Thornbushes

Nelson Mandela, first black president of South Africa, tells how as a child he once lost face in front of his friends. He and his childhood pals delighted in playing in the hills above his early home. One day their play included climbing on and off an "unruly donkey." As Mandela jumped onto the donkey, it "bolted into a nearby thornbush," throwing him into the thornbush and badly scratching him. He was embarrassed in front of his friends. "Like the people of the East," Mandela writes in his autobiography, "Africans have a highly developed sense of dignity, or what the Chinese call 'face.' I had lost face among my friends. Even though it was a donkey that unseated me, I learned that to humiliate another person is to make him suffer an unnecessarily cruel fate." For Mandela, this was a lesson for life. Even as a boy, he reports, he would not dishonor his opponents.[34]

Face was an issue in the first post-Eden conflict recorded in Scripture (Gen. 4:1-16). When Abel's offering was accepted by God and Cain's not, Cain's face fell. At least two different translations of what lay behind this expression have been offered. The first is that "Cain was very angry." The second is that he was "deeply troubled."[35] Both are possible responses to the loss of face. In any event, murder followed. Cain rejected God's counsel to recover face by doing well.

Face is a powerful motivator of human behavior. James Gilligan observes that "the emotion of shame is the primary or ultimate cause of all violence, whether toward others or toward the self." He sees "the fear of shame and ridicule, and the overbearing need to prevent others from laughing at oneself by making them weep instead" as "the main motives for violence."[36] Humans will do almost anything to save face.

When in conflict, it is essential that I remember the importance of face. I can save face by showing respect and giving serious consideration to the thoughts and feelings of the other. I can best care for my own face when I take the initiative to invite honest responses, including disagreements, to my thoughts and feelings. An open face is to be wanted above a closed face.

Commitment to Being "Unconditionally Constructive"

Roger Fisher and Scott Brown, associated with the Harvard Negotiation Project, propose that persons engaging each other in conflict make a commitment to being "unconditionally constructive" before proceeding.[37] They offer this counsel not for lofty religious or philosophical reasons but simply because they believe it leads to success. It seems especially appropriate for those of us who claim the name of Christ to be "unconditionally constructive" as we enter into dialogue.

Conclusion

Theologian Reuel Howe once wrote a book called *The Miracle of Dialogue*.[38] I think he had it right. Miracles do happen when people communicate with each other in a dialogical manner. The miracle may not always be agreement, but even in disagreement, dialogical communication can hold our hearts together. Perhaps that is the greater miracle.

Discussion Questions

1. How do persons dehumanize those with whom they are in conflict? How might persons affirm partners in conflict without necessarily agreeing with them?

2. Withholding information is a way of gaining and maintaining power over another. What are appropriate and inappropriate disclosures when in conflict with another?

3. Dialogical communication is neither giving into nor dominating the other. Dialogical communication is bearing witness to the truth as I understand it, listening to the truth as the other understands it, and together pursuing a common truth. Do you agree?

4. Identify a current issue over which people disagree. What might being "tough-minded" and "tender-hearted" look like in practice as this issue is addressed? How might anger be expressed cleanly?

5. Identify interpersonal or group conflict you have recently experienced. Complete the "L Scale" assessing your own behavior in the conflict. What insights does the scale offer?

6. Share a story in which face was an issue for you. How did others care or not care for your face? What did you do to care for your face? How does the incarnation of Jesus serve as a model for how we as humans might deal constructively with conflict?

Table 2: THE L SCALE
A MEASURE OF HUMAN RELATIONSHIPS

The L Scale is a measure of your relationship with another. You may use it to evaluate a short-term or long-term relationship, or a relationship focused around a specific event or series of events. In conflict, it is a useful instrument to test one's readiness to engage another A low score may indicate a need for further personal preparation. A higher score may indicate that one is more ready to engage the other

On each item circle the number that most accurately describes your behavior in the relationship you have chosen to evaluate.

Patient	8	7	6	5	4	3	2	1	Impatient
Kind	8	7	6	5	4	3	2	1	Unkind
Envious	1	2	3	4	5	6	7	8	Accepting
Modest	8	7	6	5	4	3	2	1	Boastful
Conceited	1	2	3	4	5	6	7	8	Humble
Rude	1	2	3	4	5	6	7	8	Courteous
Insist on my way	1	2	3	4	5	6	7	8	Open to another way
Irritable	1	2	3	4	5	6	7	8	Self-Controlled
No record of wrongs	8	7	6	5	4	3	2	1	Keep score of wrongs
Sad about other's wrongs	8	7	6	5	4	3	2	1	Gloat over other's wrongs
Sad when truth prevails	1	2	3	4	5	6	7	8	Glad when truth prevails
Slow to excuse	1	2	3	4	5	6	7	8	Quick to excuse
Open to trusting the other	8	7	6	5	4	3	2	1	Closed to trusting the other
Hopeful of the other	8	7	6	5	4	3	2	1	Despair of the other
Give up quickly on the other	1	2	3	4	5	6	7	8	Persevere with the other

When completed, add all of your circled numbers and record your score.
_____Your total score (maximum of 120)

Note: The L-Scale is based on the qualities of love listed by the Apostle Paul in 1 Corinthians 13.

STRUGGLING
WITH
THE TENSION

WHEN TENSION BECOMES EVIDENT, the impulse is to find solutions as quickly as possible. Some individuals rise up like an angry bear and try to reduce the tension by intimidating others to accept the solution they prefer. Some people become like dough and try to absorb the tensions. Still others try to do some magic and make the tension disappear by denying that it exists. The greater the conflict, the more determined the reactions seem to be. The yearning for a resolution to tension is natural and important. The irony is that focusing on solutions too quickly may make the conflict worse.

Dealing with conflict is a little like being pregnant. It becomes clear at some point that the delivery needs to take place. Rushing the labor and focusing on a seemingly impossible challenge of getting a baby through a narrow birth canal makes matters worse, not better. To ease the delivery process, it helps, first of all, to understand what is going on. Understanding can bring about constructive action of mother, father, doctor, and others. Understanding and responding constructively do not entirely eliminate the pain or labor but do make the birth experience more positive.

A key step in transforming conflict is to shift the focus from finding a solution to understanding the peacemaking process. As described in previous chapters, communication is an essential part of peacemaking. The purpose of communication is to bring about understanding. Poor communication makes conflict worse. Inadequate communication adds more tensions, pain, hurtful words, and despair to the old. The result is either more hostility or a greater determination to avoid being honest, both of which can bring death to the relationship. By contrast, good communication leads to understanding, bringing people closer to one another.

Conflict transformation requires more than communication. Communication brings the tensions and issues to the surface where they can be addressed. Problem-solving and healing skills are then needed to deal with them. To understand the issues and reasons for tension is one thing; to appropriately respond to them is another.

The next four chapters look at issues related to problem solving and healing. Chapter 7 summarizes some of the contexts in which these processes take place. Chapter 8 explores some basic approaches and skills related to problem solving. Chapter 9 looks at what happens when communication goes awry and conflict turns violent. Chapter 10 examines the role of healing and forgiveness in conflict.

Problem solving and healing, when fully effective, result in far more than a solution to a problem. People are transformed, even if just a little. What was separated moves toward connectedness. The negative emotions of fear and despair are replaced with trust and hope. Tension is transformed into peace. While we may only get a glimpse of the transformation that is possible, we know in our souls this is as it should be. The goal is worthy of our efforts.

7

Choosing a Path for Conflict Transformation

By Dean E. Peachey

Dean E. Peachey lives in Kitchener, Ontario, where he makes his living as a mediator, conflict resolution trainer, and consultant for groups in conflict. He works in a wide range of settings, including congregational, workplace, and land use disputes, "with a particular interest in difficult situations that just will not go away." He has worked formally in conflict resolution for nineteen years. However, his most challenging experiences in conflict are his own— from twenty-two years of marriage, being a father, serving as a lay leader in a congregation, and being involved in the development of both nonprofit organizations and a business partnership. Increasingly, his interests lie in cultivating inner peace and nonviolence and blending conflict transformation seminars with canoeing and wilderness activities.

Maria and Jennifer

The frustration surged through every fiber in her body, and Jennifer visibly stiffened when she saw that the drawer was empty. The ledger supposed to be kept under lock and key was not there. Glancing about the office, she saw the corner of the ledger under a stack of files that formed the clutter on Maria's desk.

With deliberate steps, Jennifer strode to Maria's desk. She yanked the ledger from under the pile, noting with satisfaction that the files slid in disarray across the desk. She sat at her own desk, efficiently wrote her entries in the book, then stood abruptly and placed the book in its drawer. The drawer slammed shut, and Jennifer turned the key with a flourish.

The thick silence that blanketed the office remained until Maria left for lunch at noon. By 1:45 p.m., Maria had not returned. Jennifer remained, answering the phones and providing office coverage, her anger building with her hunger at Maria's timely retaliation. When Maria nonchalantly returned at 2:00 p.m., Jennifer strode out of the office without either of them speaking.

The relationship between the two women who shared bookkeeping duties and telephone reception for a small construction company had steadily deteriorated over the past two years. Small deeds took on greater consequence as open communication withered. Eventually each came to interpret the other person's behaviors as deliberate acts of disrespect and antagonism. Each came to believe the other was spreading gossip about her in the company.

The women complained about each other to their supervisor, who eventually called in an outside mediator. The mediator met with the women, made limited progress in resolving the conflict, and scheduled a second meeting. Before that meeting took place, Jennifer and Maria had an argument. Maria struck Jennifer in the face.

At the second meeting, Maria was a transformed person. Thoroughly shaken by her action in hitting a coworker, she had spent the past several days looking inside, trying to understand the source of her anger, facing her ability to behave in ways counter to her values and those of her family and church. Instead of blaming Jennifer for provoking her, she was resolving to make changes in her own life.

Faced with Maria's inward gaze, Jennifer was able to shift from defending and blaming to also looking at her own contributions to the conflict. Ironically, the escalation of the conflict to a crisis point had prompted the shift from blame to discovery, enabling the first steps in transforming the conflict.

From Blame to Discovery

Conflict can be a flash flood—sudden, unexpected, swirling us in a confusing, overwhelming mix of currents and debris. Other times, conflict develops almost imperceptibly, slowly chilling and hardening a relationship until there is barely a trickle of civility between the people involved. Either way, conflict transformation is a tall order. Whether the conflict is a raging torrent or the big chill, positive transformation of the conflict often feels impossible. We dimly know that with God all things are possible, but how can this knowledge be made practical in conflict?

Genuine transformation of the conflict—as compared to striking a compromise, or imposing a solution—becomes possible when we move from blame to discovery. This shift from blaming ourselves, other people, circumstances, or God for the conflict requires deliberate choice. When we choose to use the conflict as an opportunity for discovery, it can indeed deepen our understanding of ourselves, our relationships with the other people in the conflict, and of God. Transformation made practical has two parts: transformation of self and transformation of the relationship in conflict.

Transforming the Self

> "Why do you see the speck in your neighbor's eye, but do not notice the log in your own eye? Or how can you say to your neighbor, 'Let me take the speck out of your eye,' while the log is in your own eye? You hypocrite, first take the log out of your own eye, and then you will see clearly to take the speck out of your neighbor's eye." (Matt. 7:3-5)

The primary and toughest part of conflict transformation is transforming myself (or allowing myself to be transformed). Conflict reveals to us who we are, and we may not like what we see. In conflict we see that we are capable of feeling resentful, insecure, fearful, powerless, angry, or hateful—and of acting on these feelings. An attitude of discovery will enable us to look inside ourselves, and see what is there—good, bad, and painfully ugly.

As we begin to discover and acknowledge sources of conflict inside us, we can respond differently in conflict. It has often been said that war begins in the human heart. While that statement does not capture the whole truth, our inner states often contribute to the conflict.

I so quickly blame others for *making* me angry, or *making* me feel anxious, instead of launching a discovery of what is in my own life that leads me to be anxious or angry. People who state, "She always has to be in control," are probably saying as much about themselves as about the other. A more accurate statement might be, "In this meeting I don't have as much control as *I* would like to have."

Jesus' urging to deal first with the log in our own eye is often dismissed as an exaggeration. It is not. It is profound and practical advice because amid conflict our own behavior is what we have the greatest chance of changing. Too often, however, in the search for something "easier" to deal with, we expend enormous energy trying to alter the circumstances or remake another individual. Of course most such effort is futile since other people readily resist attempts to change them!

Amid his struggle to liberate the people of India from colonial rule, Gandhi is reported to have said, "I have only three enemies. My favorite enemy, the one most easily influenced for the better, is the British Empire. My second enemy, the Indian people, is far more difficult. But my most formidable opponent is a man named Mohandas K. Gandhi. With him I seem to have very little influence."

Understanding the self is only the first step in transforming it. Cultivating the inner life with a sense of personal strength, "centeredness," and balance is essential to handling conflict well. I can't expect to function well in conflict if I am overworking, over-worrying, or otherwise out of balance. Nor can I expect to transform conflict if the pursuit of this world's goods or achievements has choked out my spiritual path like the encroaching thorns in Jesus' parable of the farmer sowing seed.

Although the skills for communication and problem solving described in this book are important, they are not the starting point for practical peacemaking. Living and working well with conflict is first about who we are as people, rather than about a particular set of skills and strategies. Regular time devoted to deepening a spiritual life and building physical and emotional health is critical to being able to use conflict as an opportunity for discovery. Prayer and meditation are vital preparation for engaging in conflict. A short burst of prayer when a conflict escalates is no substitute for a regular spiritual discipline.

Transforming the Relationship

Conflict also is an opportunity for discovery in the relationships among the people in conflict. Indeed, conflict provides us with the "moment of truth" in relationships. An auto collision or a mugging can suddenly change the relationship of strangers (indifference) to one of conflict. It poses for us the question of do I care for this person apart from his or her role as the person who smashed my car or robbed me?

On a daily basis, conflict poses a similar question for us at home, on the job, or in church: How committed am I to working things out with this person who is different from me? Am I willing to transform a relationship of advocacy and opposition to one of coexistence or partnership? Can I ask God to give me the eyes to see antagonists as potential friends?

In 1993, sworn enemies Yitzhak Rabin, Prime Minister of Israel, and Yasser Arafat, leader of the Palestine Liberation Organization, stood together on the lawn of the White House to give their assent to a peace plan. Each man had been sharply criticized by his own people for meeting with the enemy and formally recognizing the other side. Facing the criticism, Prime Minister Rabin observed, "You don't make peace with your friends; you make peace with your enemies." It is a simple statement that reflects a profound attitude, and one that subsequently cost Rabin his life at the hands of an assassin who did not believe that enemies could or should become friends.

Transforming the relationship does not mean that all is forgotten, or that anything is forgiven. It does not mean that the issues are resolved. What it does mean is that you are prepared to shift the conflict from a contest to be won to a problem to be solved. You are ready to work together on the difficult task of resolving the issues as fully as they can be resolved. If they can't be resolved, you are prepared to agree on ways to limit the disagreements so that they do not escalate or rage out of control.

Responding to Various Levels of Tension

When Tension Is Low

When the tension level in the conflict is *relatively low*, the process of transforming the relationship can be initiated by anyone in the conflict. An important key to working with low-level tension is to act on the discomfort you are experiencing. The difficulty in sleeping well, the momentary tensing you experience when you hear your coworker's footsteps approaching, or the sudden impatience when your spouse criticizes you are all valuable signals that something is amiss. They deserve attention.

Often the biggest obstacle to transforming conflict is the desire to avoid or ignore it. Sometimes we avoid dealing with conflict because the issue is minor; we do not want to appear to be petty or picky. But those little piles of dirt can grow into mountains over time if ignored.

In each situation, ask yourself whether either the issue or the relationship is important to you. If the answer to both parts of the question is "no," it is appropriate to ignore the incident. For example, a disrespectful gesture from a stranger on the street need not lead to a problem-solving discussion. But because an important relationship is at stake, a family member's tone of voice that sets you on edge can be worth addressing. This points to the need to deal with low-level tension quickly and regularly.

Take time to reflect on what the inner sources of this conflict are for you, then open communication with the other person. Finally, by using the suggestions on listening, speaking, dialogue, problem solving, and forgiveness provided in Chapters 4–6, 8, and 10, you will often be able to handle the differences in a positive fashion.

When Tension Is Medium Level

When the tension level rises to *medium level*, communication usually becomes difficult. People's goals typically shift from solving the original problem to winning, being proven right, or preserving face and reputation.

Transforming the self and the relationship in medium-intensity conflicts requires conscious and sustained effort. Training or coaching for the people may be necessary, and a more objective third party such as a mediator can be very useful. At this mid-level stage, a friend or colleague from the setting may be able to serve adequately in the mediator role. Signals that it is time to involve a third party in a conflict may include the following:

- People are at an impasse on the issues;
- Trust is broken;
- Communication is distorted/broken;
- The conflict is escalating or becoming destructive;
- Significant power imbalances make achieving a fair resolution difficult.

A mediator helps individuals in conflict clearly identify the issues, communicate about what is most important to them, and explore options for resolving the conflict. *The one thing a mediator cannot do is decide the outcome or impose a settlement.* Typically the mediator will first talk separately with each party, then bring everyone together to untangle communication, share perspectives, and explore solutions. Mediation is a problem-solving approach that focuses not on who is right or wrong, but on developing a satisfactory and lasting solution to difficult conflicts. Mediation when the tension is at a medium level is often informal in nature.

Informal Mediation

Mediation can be informal or formal. Informal mediation is done routinely by friends, supervisors, pastors, and relatives. The informal mediator's work is an extension of his or her relationship to those in conflict. Because informal mediators are often connected to the people in conflict, an informal mediator may not always be completely neutral. Most important is that the informal mediator be seen as fair and credible by the people in conflict. The informal mediator may have certain preferred outcomes but will need to be prepared to put them aside to allow those most affected by the issue to build their own resolution.

It is easy for an informal mediator to be sucked into an unhelpful pattern. This happens when the mediator becomes the third corner of a triangle: where Jennifer talks to a third person about a problem with Maria—but does not address the issue directly with Maria. A good response to Jennifer's complaint is to ask, "What happens when you talk to Maria about this?" If Jennifer replies that she has not discussed it with Maria, it is usually appropriate to encourage her to do so before involving others in the dispute.

It may take some urging for Jennifer to discuss the situation with Maria, as many of us prefer to avoid conflict or wait for someone else to solve the problem for us. Sometimes cultural norms against talking directly to the person with whom one has a disagreement may need to be respected. But in most North American settings, far more damage is done by lack of direct communication.

If Jennifer insists that it just is not possible for her to approach Maria directly, the informal mediator can offer to meet with the two of them. At the meeting the informal mediator can set guidelines for communication and use constructive procedures for problem solving.

Informal mediators who know the people in conflict have the advantage of understanding the context for the interaction. They can draw on their positive history with the parties to encourage them to engage in a process of discovery.

At the same time, informal mediators should be aware of hazards they face. One is the danger of becoming more eager for resolution than the people in conflict. When this happens, the informal mediator can readily succumb to the temptation to feel responsible for the outcome rather than letting people take responsibility for agreeing or not.

Because of the potential for an informal mediator to become entangled in the conflict, a mediation team can be used. This may be especially desirable if the conflict involves difficult issues or significant power differences between the participants.

When Tension Is High

In conflict situations involving *high tension*, informal mediation becomes less appropriate. As the tension escalates, it is less likely that anyone associated with the conflict or the people in it will be seen as fair. The risk to the informal mediator, or anyone inside the group in which the conflict is occurring, also increases dramatically. Many pastors or job supervisors have been "burned" in such situations when angry people turn their frustration at the mediator or blame unresolved conflict on the person trying to help. High intensity conflict deserves outside assistance such as a professional mediator or independent arbitrator. Mediation when the tension is at a high level is often formal in nature.

Formal Mediation

More formal mediation is provided by someone independent of the situation and who often has specialized experience or training in mediation. Such mediators come from a wide range of backgrounds. Depending on their position, they may work on either a volunteer or paid basis. Skilled volunteers are available through local schools or community mediation centers or sometimes through denominational services. Paid mediators may work in either a private or government office or do mediation along with a counseling or law practice. The telephone directory's "Yellow Pages" carry listings of mediators, and some states and provinces have mediation associations that offer assistance in locating an appropriate mediator.

Third-Party Decision Makers: Arbitration and Legal Action

Another option is the intervention of an authority figure who can make an appropriate decision to settle the dispute. This can happen informally, such as when a senior leader in an organization makes a decision, or more formally through arbitration. Relying on an authority figure, or using arbitration, in which the outside neutral person makes a final decision, usually does little to transform the relationship or the individuals. But it can be better than having the conflict linger and fester. Arbitration is usually done by professionals who are knowledgeable in the area of the dispute (construction, contracts, and so forth).

It has been said that "going to court is like losing a cow to save a calf." Most people are well aware of the costs in time, money, and emotional energy of waging a legal battle. In addition, some Christian traditions avoid the use of secular courts because of the coercive powers the courts exercise, and because of Jesus' teachings on direct resolution of disputes between believers.

Many people live their entire lives without ever being involved in a court action. However, most people can benefit at one time or another from sound legal advice. Dismissing an employee, challenging a landlord who is not maintaining the property, or developing a business partnership are just a few examples of the many situations that have significant legal implications. Timely advice from a lawyer can prevent harmful and unnecessary conflicts. A lawyer can advise you not only of what the law might state, but also of social norms or common practices that might be relevant to your situation.

There are times when a legal action is appropriate, such as when the conflict is about legal issues or legal interpretation. It may also be necessary when one party refuses to participate in mediation or when mediation has been unsuccessful. Legal action may be required if the goal is to challenge an unjust law or policy or to set a social or legal precedent.

If your situation involves any of the above, you will need to decide whether to engage in a formal court action. In making such a decision, remember that the lawyer's role is to give you advice, not to tell you what to do. A good lawyer will present information and options and then allow you to make the decision. In making the decision, be sure to get the candid advice of good friends and church leaders.

Being Helpful When Others Are in Conflict

When you observe a friend or family member in conflict, you can do several things to help transform the conflict. First, remember it is the other person's conflict to handle, not yours. Do not take on more responsibility for a resolution than the people who are in conflict.

Second, listen to the person fully and carefully. Through careful listening you will come to a better understanding of your friend's situation. Sometimes providing this "listening ear" is all that is required for your friend to think through what she needs to do in the situation.

Third, once your friend knows you really understand his experience, you can ask if he would like your help exploring the conflict. If the answer is yes, only at that point may it be time to gently invite your friend to look inward to discover internal sources of the conflict.

Fourth, based on the level of tension in the conflict, you can discuss possible paths (direct dialogue, informal mediation, formal mediation) that your friend might select to transform the conflict.

Conclusion

Practical peacemaking becomes more challenging as the tension level of a conflict rises. As in any other aspect of life, practicing conflict transformation can yield the experience to deal with progressively more challenging situations. It is important to practice transformation with the daily conflicts that occur with low levels of tension, rather than avoiding them or forcing our own way. To do otherwise is to lose valuable opportunities for both inner discovery and skill development. As we deepen our spiritual walk through conflict, our skills will grow as well.

Informal mediation provides an opportunity to strengthen our connection with other people and continue transformation in more intense conflicts. But caution and responsible relationships require that we seek outside assistance when it is appropriate to do so.

In Matthew 18, Jesus urges us to make repeated efforts to work things out when there is a conflict. When the first approach does not work, Jesus says try something else, and involve another person. If that does not work, try again, involving more people. These verses speak of the role for other people in the dispute, but even more importantly, they speak of the importance of persistently desiring transformation and not giving ourselves the option of quitting simply because I tried, but the other person did not initially respond the way I wanted him or her to respond.

Discussion Questions

1. How are you first aware of tension in yourself? What physical sensations are involved? What do you tend to do when you are tense?

2. If you could change one thing about your reaction to conflict, what would it be?

3. Think of conflict you experienced in which tension was relatively low, medium, and high. Did you respond differently? Would outside involvement have helped?

4. Do you know of anyone who has been involved in informal mediation, mediation, arbitration, or court? Did it help resolve the conflict? Would they do it again?

5. Do you think Christians ought to take legal action? If so, when and for what reason? If not, why not?

6. Have you ever tried to help a friend or family member in conflict? What did you say or do? Was it helpful? What would you do similarly? What would you do differently?

8

Keys to
Problem Solving

Lawrence E. Ressler

Lawrence grew up in a non-Mennonite community in southern Ohio, where his Mennonite parents were involved in church planting with Appalachian people. His appreciation for diversity has been enriched by living in Ohio, Mississippi, Virginia, Pennsylvania, and Kentucky as well as working in colleges affiliated with five different denominations: Mennonite, Evangelical Friends, Brethren in Christ, Southern Baptist, and Free Methodist. Lawrence has worked as a mediator and family therapist for fifteen years. Among rich conflict experiences, he has led a court-mandated seminar on conflict resolution for more than 1,000 individuals who filed for divorce or wanted a custody change for their children. Lawrence is currently professor of social work at Roberts Wesleyan College in Rochester, New York.

Why Can't We Be Normal

On several occasions I intervened in squabbles of our children and neighborhood friends, using what I thought was good conflict resolution process. I invited all to sit and tell their version of what was going on. I asked them to paraphrase what they heard another person say. Each person got a turn, no interruptions allowed. After each had a turn, I helped them identify the issues. We tried to take each issue and suggest several different ways to resolve it. We then explored which seemed best. After they agreed on ways to settle the issues, I tried to make sure they were feeling positive about each other. Then I permitted them to continue playing.

When neighbors returned home after such an intervention, my daughter and son said, "We hate when you do that. It embarrasses us. Nobody else does it this way. We just want to be normal."

101

Commonsense Problem Solving

There is often a significant gap between our desire to resolve conflict constructively and our ability to do so. In theory, a few simple and easy steps should solve conflicts. But of course what is simple in theory can be hard to put into practice. Here are a few basic initial principles.

There Is More than One Way to Solve a Problem

A key problem-solving principle is that there is not just one way forward. Five strategies can easily be identified: collaboration, compromise, forcing, accommodation, and avoidance. Collaboration occurs when those in conflict seek a mutual and fully satisfying solution. Compromise involves working together for a solution that gives all some of what they want and no one all of what they want. Forcing takes place when one person insists on his or her way. Accommodating involves giving others what they want. Avoidance attempts to deal with conflict by ignoring it.

Different Situations Require Different Approaches

A second commonsense principle is that one approach does not work for all conflict. At times individuals need to sit down, discuss issues, and reach a fully agreeable solution. In other situations, as full agreement proves elusive, the best solution may be compromise. There are times forcing may be necessary for safety or to uphold certain values or principles. There are also occasions in which accommodating to the interests of others is most appropriate. Finally, it can be useful to postpone dealing with conflict until there is a better time, place, and emotional atmosphere to deal with issues.

Each approach can be destructive when used excessively or at the wrong time. As good as collaboration is, expecting to collaborate on all matters is unhealthy as well as exhausting. Family therapists call this enmeshment. Likewise, compromise can be problematic. It is not appropriate to compromise on safety issues, for example. Overuse of accommodation can lead to a sense of emptiness and enable inappropriate actions by others. Forcing one's will on others will limit their development and may stir various forms of rebellion. Avoidance, which tries to deal with conflict by ignoring it, will eventually result in the death of the relationship or in pressure which builds to the point of explosion.

Working Together Is Better

While all of the approaches have their own time and place, collaborating and compromising have strengths over forcing, accommodating, and avoiding. Although the latter strategies may be more efficient and seem less stressful in the short run, collaboration and compromise have the potential to bring about a more satisfying and longer-lasting solution and to build relationship.

There Is a Difference between How and What We Decide

It is useful to distinguish between *how* we decide and *what* we decide. The difference is subtle but important. There are four possible outcomes to conflict. The outcome may be what I want, what you want, what we both want, or what neither of us wants. It may seem that the list of outcomes is the same as the list of approaches. Getting what I want may seem similar to forcing. Giving you what you want may seem the same as accommodating. Getting what we both want may look like collaboration. Having neither of us get what we want may seem identical to avoidance.

They are not the same, however. Persons in conflict can agree through collaboration to do what I want or what you want. They can also agree to disagree. What is important is reaching the decision together. A person in conflict can also use forcing to get various outcomes. A supervisor, for example, can insist on his own way, that a subordinate make the decision, or that the issue be silenced.

How We Decide Can Be More Important than What We Decide

Positive outcomes require positive process. Poor process will nearly always have a negative impact on the outcome. Parent and teen conflict, for example, is frequently about who makes decisions as much as what the outcome is. Parents may feel they have the right and responsibility to control their children's behavior. Teens may feel they have a right and responsibility to make their own decisions. The two may actually arrive at the same outcome, but the struggle over who gets to make the decision may so sour the relationship that the outcome becomes unimportant. While using the most appropriate approach does not guarantee that the outcomes will be easy or satisfactory, using the wrong approach makes outcomes more problematic.

Focus on Interests, Not Positions

It is important to keep in mind that the interests people have are different than positions they may take. Interests reflect intentions and hopes which many people can share. They are future-oriented and dynamic. Positions are conclusions people come to about issues. They tend to be personal and fixed. Discussions about positions tend to result in people feeling personally threatened and defensive, whereas discussions about interests often help people discover similarities. Focusing on interests allows individuals to seek shared solutions to common interests.

Steps to Conflict Problem Solving

The problem-solving process involves a few rather simple steps. The steps are easy to follow as long as people remain calm and issues are less important. When tension rises, the steps are more difficult to keep in mind. A trick to resolving difficult conflict is to slow down and follow the next steps carefully and deliberately.

Make Time

The first concrete step in resolving conflict is to set aside time to deal with the issues. The more regular the times, the less the stress and more manageable the process. Regular church meetings, regular spouse conversations, and regular family meetings help keep conflicts from becoming major crises.

Allow Each Person to Talk (Make Sure Everyone Else Is Listening)

The second step is to make sure all participants have opportunity to share their perspective. The goal must be to understand each other, not to change people's minds or demand a solution. "No interruptions" should be one firm rule. The more difficult the issue, the more each person needs to work at listening. Paraphrasing helps focus attention on what the speaker is trying to say.

Identify the Issues Creating Tension

Often solutions are hard to achieve because many issues are contributing to the tension. Effort must be made to identify participants' multiple underlying interests. A challenge is to avoid shifting the focus to positions which have been held in the past, exist at present, or might be taken in the future. It is useful to make as complete a list of issues as possible before focusing on a specific issue.

Where there has been ongoing conflict, it may be necessary to spend time discussing past hurts. Frequently such pain remains so present that today's issues cannot be dealt with clearly and directly. If the pain of the past is not addressed, past, present, and future become thoroughly confused. Then constructive resolution is almost impossible. At this point, simply listing the issues from the past is satisfactory. They, along with current issues, can be addressed when the list is complete.

Often people will at various points along the way internally identify other important issues. Such issues should be welcomed and added to the list when thought of. The initial list should be seen not as complete but as an evolving basis from which to address the conflict.

Work Together One Issue at a Time

Once the list is made, it is wise to focus on each issue individually. All involved should have opportunity to share thoughts and feelings, to clarify what they are saying and why it is important. Sometimes writing for a few minutes helps collect initial thoughts. With good communication, reasons for tension and the nature of the differences will become clearer.

Identify Options and Choose the Best

After hearing one another's concerns about an issue, the group can begin to think creatively about options for resolution. Together, list as many options as possible. Then choose the options workable for all involved. Where full agreement is impossible, consider compromise. Where compromise is not forthcoming, see if the preference of the other person is more prudent than your own. Together examine pros and cons. Aim to reach agreement on an outcome even if it is not your preferred one.

Keep the overall pattern in mind. Aim to balance outcomes between your preference and preferences of others. When one person continues to get his or her way, the other person usually becomes resentful or loses interest. When no resolution can be found for the moment, agree to disagree. Should there be no agreement, agree to address concerns again later.

Be Committed to Work Together

A determination to work together and to reach some type of agreement is critical. Even if there is some discomfort with the resolution, agree to try it for a while, then re-evaluate it. As the discussion concludes, it is helpful to shift the focus to the relationship, which is more important than any specific solution. To agree is a wonderful thing. To agree to disagree can also be wonderful because the differences have not destroyed the relationship. If comfortable to everyone, you may want to close with prayer, asking for God's blessing and for forgiveness for any harmful words and shortcomings.

It's Not That Simple:
Critical Ingredients for Problem Solving

Walter and Elaine

Walter and Elaine's relationship had problems from the beginning. Arguments and mean words were more common than laughter. Suspicion and despair set in. They stayed together for a few years, but there was little goodness in the marriage.

The one thing they did have in common was deep love for son Daniel. The main reason they married was Elaine's pregnancy. Both Walter and Elaine bonded to their child immediately and deeply.

They didn't want to divorce and went to a counselor, but this seemed to make little difference. Tensions rose so high that the most constructive action they could take was to separate. That was when the real problems began. Who would care for their son?

Elaine argued that Daniel should stay with her. The mother and child relationship, she believed, was critical for his development. Furthermore, she did not trust Walter's parenting. She claimed he had a quick temper and was insensitive to Daniel's needs. Elaine was afraid Walter would become abusive. Two weekends a month and one evening a week were enough visitation for Walter, she believed. She also wanted the right to make any legal parenting decisions because the two of them had such difficulty making decisions together.

Walter was furious. He saw the arrangement as an attempt to deny him a significant relationship with his son. He dearly loved Daniel and believed he should have at least equal access. He wanted what was best for his Daniel, and that included a generous amount of time together.

Walter felt the comments about his temper were intentionally exaggerated to deny him his rights. In fact, he thought he should have the most time with Daniel and legal custody because he was the healthier of the two. Elaine, he believed, was unstable emotionally and did not discipline Daniel. She was overprotective because she had grown up in a home with an alcoholic mother. Furthermore, he had a stable job but believed Elaine would likely end up on welfare.

When Elaine received a letter from Walter's attorney indicating that Walter would try to get primary physical and legal custody, she was certain he was doing this for spite, to get back at her. Walter had never had an interest in Daniel before and was always working. This was an example of how mean he could be. Walter knew Daniel was the only one in the world she really cared about. If she lost Daniel, she could not go on. She would fight for him with every penny she had.

Wisdom

Simple conflict is simple to solve. Difficult conflict is not. The problem is not that the theory is incorrect or the steps inappropriate. The problem is that real-life conflict can be incredibly complex. We quickly find ourselves confused about where to begin and what to do. We become defensive or angry. When we talk, the words get tangled up. We get hurt and find it difficult to listen. We don't always know what is healthy and morally appropriate. The conflicts we face in life sometimes make the theory and the easy steps seem useless. Then we need not theory or more steps—but wisdom.

When we think of wise problem solvers, Solomon comes to mind. Solomon's wisdom is illustrated in his handling of one of the most complex areas of human conflict: child custody. Two prostitutes living together each bore a child. One child died. Both claimed the living child was theirs. Solomon was asked to help solve what seemed an impossible situation.

He asked each woman to tell her story. Then, using a clever method, he discovered who the true mother was. When he asked the two to divide the baby in half, the real mother's love forced her to prefer to give the baby up rather than kill it. The people of Israel were awed by Solomon's ability to solve the problem (1 Kings 3:16-28).

The most significant lessons about Solomon's wisdom, however, come earlier in the story, when young Solomon is about to be anointed king. In a prayer to God, he says,

> "I am only a little child; I do not know how to go out or come in. And your servant is in the midst of the people whom you have chosen, a great people, so numerous they cannot be numbered or counted. Give your servant therefore an understanding mind to govern your people, able to discern between good and evil; for who can govern this your great people?" It pleased the Lord that Solomon had asked this. God said to him, "Because you have asked this, and have not asked for yourself long life or riches, or for the life of your enemies, but have asked for yourself understanding to discern what is right, I now do according to your word. Indeed I give you a wise and discerning mind; no one like you has been before you and no one like you shall arise after you. (1 Kings 3:7b-12)

When we face complex conflict, it may help to remember that Solomon was not always keenly discerning and confident. Early in life Solomon felt confused and overwhelmed. In his own words, he did not know how to go out or come in. The most critical point of the passage was that what he most wanted was a discerning mind. Pleased with Solomon's priorities, God granted his request.

One of the most important things we can do when seeking solutions to conflict is to acknowledge the complexity of the situation and admit our confusion. Dealing with complex conflict requires humility, openness, and a persistent desire for wisdom. If the yearning is genuine, like Solomon's, it will grow into wisdom. The solutions will become evident—though perhaps only in time.

Use the Tension Productively

Key to dealing with conflict is to become comfortable with the tension that exists. Tension may feel uncomfortable but is not bad. It tells us that something is not right and gets us to pay attention to a problem. Tension is a little like hunger. Hunger is an uncomfortable feeling that reminds us we need nourishment and directs our attention to food. It motivates us to eat and keeps us alive. Tension, like hunger, beckons us to act. As odd as it may seem, tension in conflict is a necessary part of peacemaking.

Emory's Fury

Emory was angry. Something needed to be done. The family had spent the day at his brother's house, and the cousins were having a great time. Emory and Jean had waited until the latest possible moment before leaving for home, an hour away. When they told the kids it was time to go, they refused to come because the game they were playing was not over. Emory insisted. The kids made derogatory comments in front of others. The children, he felt, needed to be taught a lesson. Disrespect to parents would not be tolerated.

Normally he would have let them have it once they got in the car. They would be grounded or possibly have their allowance withheld for the month. They would get a good scolding. The drive would be a sad ending to a wonderful day.

This time he decided to change his approach. He would tell the children in controlled tones that he was angry at the way they had acted. He wanted all to share what they were feeling and thinking. The next person needed to repeat what the previous person said.

The kids pointed out they had no warning and were in the middle of a game. They felt pushed around by adults and disrespected. It would have been better if they had been given a half-hour warning. The parents expressed frustration with the derogatory comments the children had made and their lack of responsiveness.

The hour-long drive went quickly as each shared thoughts and feelings. Rather than finishing the day in painful separation, they ended with a solution all eagerly agreed to. The next time the parents would give a half-hour warning. The kids would leave without protest when the time was up. Everyone was satisfied.

The most basic adjustment for many people is to understand that tension is a God-given and necessary part of life. The more uncomfortable we are with tension, the more likely we are to attack the other, to jump to conclusions, and to act prematurely and harmfully. The more uptight we become, the harder it is to talk, to think, or to listen. When we relax and embrace the tension, we can explore why it exists. We can more easily control our voices and choose our words. We can listen better to what is being said and keep our defenses from getting in the way.

The Critical Role of Respect

A critical ingredient for achieving resolution is respect. Where there is no respect, there is no hope for a constructive solution. When respect remains high throughout the process, a positive resolution to the conflict will nearly always emerge, even if it is to agree to disagree.

> "Teacher, which commandment in the law is the greatest?" He [Jesus] said to him, "'You shall love the Lord your God with all your heart, and with all your soul, and with all your mind.' This is the greatest and first commandment. And a second is like it: 'You shall love your neighbor as yourself.' On these two commandments hang all the law and the prophets." (Matt. 22:36-40)

Three types of respect are critical: respect for others, respect for self, and respect for God. Respect for others means we are concerned about the impact on them. It is important to understand that respect for others is not the same as agreeing with them. Respect for others means recognizing that they are created in the image of God, that they must be treated with dignity, and that they have a right to their own thoughts, feelings, and perspectives.

While the Scriptures clearly warn of the danger of pride, this does not mean we should have no self-respect. We are, after all, created in the image of God. Without self-respect, we cannot respect others.

Respect for God helps keep us humble. Being aware that God alone is in control can help us relax and keep perspective on the future, since we are not charged with ultimate responsibility.

Have the Right Attitude

There are a number of destructive attitudes people can have in conflict. Revenge is a popular one. "An eye for an eye" is a common way to want to deal with tension. I want you to feel the pain I feel. I want you to hurt as I do. Rather than resolve conflict, some prefer to get even and may wait years to do so. As long as the desire for revenge persists, the conflict will remain alive.

Repression, or desire to ignore the past, is another frequent attitude in conflict. For some, the pain is greater than their energy to deal with the issues. For others, lack of hope that anything will change has settled in. As long as there is no willingness to deal openly with tension and feelings, conflict will persist.

Conflict can only be transformed with a determined and positive attitude. Although helplessness and negative thinking are usually mixed in, deep in the soul must be interest in transforming tension into a healthy, respectful, and workable solution. The greater the tension, the more important the attitude. This point seems simple enough, but tension can do funny things to attitude, especially if conflict persists over time. "Seek peace, and pursue it," says the Psalmist (34:14b).

Conclusion

Constructive problem solving begins with a desire for a discerning heart. It requires an understanding of what conflict is and how it works. It involves an appreciation of tension and the willingness to use it constructively. With respect for others, self, and God in our souls, we select the most appropriate process. Finally, and only then, will we be able constructively to resolve the issues.

Discussion Questions

1. On a scale of 1-10 (10 being totally wise, 1 completely lost), how would you rate yourself in knowing what to do when you are in conflict? How well did those you grew up with handle conflict? How conflict-wise are those with whom you currently associate at home, work, church?

2. Think of tension with another. When were you first aware of it? What were the earliest signs? What was causing the tension? What were

you caring about? Do you think the other person felt the tension? What were they caring about?

3. When you feel tension with another person, what is your first impulse? Do you agree that tension is a useful voice, a God-given dynamic, and an opportunity?

4. Which are you better at: respecting self, respecting others, or respecting God? What do you do when someone does not respect you? How does lack of self-respect make conflict more difficult?

5. What process do you and those you are close to use most often: agreeing, compromising, forcing, accommodating, or avoiding? What process did you experience most often when growing up? Were the individuals satisfied with the process?

6. Who tends to get their way when you have differences with those you are close to: my way, their way, we meet halfway, we don't decide, we discover a way we both like? If you could change the pattern, which would occur more and which less?

9

When Conflict Turns Violent

Ann Shenk Wenger

Ann Shenk Wenger grew up in the affectionate rough-and-tumble world of a large family in Pennsylvania. She remembers the sometimes-confusing lessons about conflict which she learned at church listening to sermons and observing business meetings. She was fortunate enough to marry Hans Wenger, the "boy next door." The next two decades were spent raising Rob, Susan, and Justina, and getting a degree in psychology. Along the way she trained as a mediator, read more books than she really had time for, and took employment in a psychiatric hospital. Ann is Director of No Longer Alone ministries, a service to individuals and families experiencing mental illness.

Jason

Jason was a new client in the adolescent area of the psychiatric facility where I worked. One day a dangerous craft needle was discovered concealed in his clothing. Despite attempts to persuade him to surrender the item, it became clear he would not give it up. Several staff took hold of Jason to take the item.

Only then did the strength in his lean body become evident. Jason thrashed about as we tried to hold him, and we were thrown about with him. In time he was restrained and the needle taken from him. Jason ended up in seclusion. The encounter left me in intense physical pain which lasted six weeks. What else could we have done? All in the situation believed they were doing what they had to.

One year later Jason was with us again. I was again called to help in a conflict with him. Violence again appeared imminent. Surrounded by staff, Jason was daring them to take him on. This time we stood back and were patient. The staff took turns talking with him.

Eventually the source of his distress became clear. It was Easter weekend and there he was in the facility. His family had canceled their planned visit—again.

Though he maintained a defiant stance, tears began to roll down Jason's cheeks. Everyone became quiet. We waited to see what Jason would do next. In our experience with him, sadness could quickly be transformed into anger and destructive aggression. This time the silence was broken not by a roar of anger but by a staff person who shared a memory of spending Easter in a foster home. Although Jason snarled that this was different, he allowed one of the men to edge closer and hand him a tissue. Soon he was calm enough to walk to a safe room.

What made the difference? Time spent together had created tentative trust. Jason had learned that we truly did have his best interests at heart. We also had more trust in ourselves and in the process of talking. This is why we stretched the encounter to give resolution a chance. Staff members were able to look beneath the scary behavior to see the scared lad and his anguish. The slower pace had allowed some staff to pray. If they were not perhaps the most articulate prayers, they were certainly heartfelt.

Most of us hope never to be in violent conflict, but violence doesn't ask permission. It is good to think ahead about our reactions to violence. It helpful as well to be able to recognize the many forms of violence.

Kinds of Violence

It is tempting to define violence as a physical act that results in physical harm. Clearly such an act is violent, but violence is also much broader. Violence is the wrongful forcing of one's will on another. It is the use of fear or pain to accomplish what one cannot accomplish by persuasion. Violence as well as its results can be more than physical. Furthermore, violence can take place in varying degrees.

Tongue and Language As Instruments of Violence

A vivid picture of violence can be found in the book of James.

> The tongue is a fire. The tongue is placed among our members as a world of iniquity; it stains the whole body, sets on fire the cycle of nature, and is itself set on fire by hell. For every species of beast and bird, of reptile and sea creature, can be tamed and has been tamed by the human species, but no one can tame the tongue—a restless evil, full of deadly poison. (Jas. 3:6-7)

The power of language, intended and able to bring us together, can be used to drive someone away, to damage a soul, and to ruin a reputation.

Violent Touch

Physical touch, which God intended for great good, can also be turned into a weapon. Touch, meant to increase bonds of affection and trust, may be used as an expression of hate or control and can destroy trust forever. An unwelcome caress on the cheek is little different from a slap. Hands meant to heal can be used to hurt and harm.

Violent touch does not necessarily require physical contact. There are many ways to threaten that serve the same purpose. An intimidating person can detain someone unwillingly by grabbing an arm, blocking a doorway, or simply leaning against the doorjamb with clear readiness to block it. The suggestion of force is often as effective as its use and may be particularly hard to identify.

Sources of Violence

It would be comforting to think that violence is something outside of ourselves, but the impulse is in each of us. If we are honest, and if we broaden our awareness of the nature of violence, we realize our own capacity for aggression. There are a number of causes.

Pat

Pat had a lot going for her. But she held others at bay with hostility and a sharp tongue. These usually did the job for her, but occasionally she would add minor acts of violence. She had been restricted to her room for shoving another client, and I stopped by to talk with her. Pat felt guilt for her attack yet chafed under the consequence she had been fully aware she would face.

"Why did you do it, Pat?" I asked.

She drew herself up to her full, not very considerable, height. "Look at me," she demanded, waving her hands at her slight frame, "I have to teach them not to mess with me!"

Violence often results from a sense of fear. When we experience a threat, one of our first instincts is to lash out. The reaction produced by the body in the face of threat is aptly labeled the "fight-or-flight" reaction. Rapid heartbeat, accelerated breathing, and the flow of adrenaline are nearly the same whether we are reacting to aggression or initiating it, and one can easily lead to the other. In the vicious cycle of violence, fear of being attacked can easily lead to being an attacker instead.

Ted

My friend Ted was a great puzzle to me. He was a Christian with many fine qualities and ideals but would sometimes subject his wife and children to painful tongue-lashings. He would focus on something they had done or not done, but I knew that couldn't be the whole story. Those same actions would usually only draw a mild or even humorous remark from him. Why did he sometimes react with such outrage?

Slowly a pattern emerged. When Ted felt guilty or inadequate, the force of his feelings was turned outward toward his family. Anger he could understand; anger he could deal with. He didn't like it, but it made sense to him that if he felt a powerful painful emotion, it must be anger. Guilt was another story; guilt he could not bear. By substituting anger, Ted shifted to a familiar emotion, and effectively cut off confrontation about the actions he feared would bring him blame.

Violence can also take place to gain respect. Fear of being disrespected for some people is as critical as the fear of being physically attacked. This is the case in some cultures more than others. It is impossible to fully know what will be considered an insult or provocation in every culture. It is possible, however, for us to be aware that differences exist, to be nondefensive when told we have caused offense, and to be willing to extend the benefit of the doubt when someone else has inadvertently pushed our buttons.

Aggression rarely stands by itself; it is an expression of something else. People who cannot bear feelings of sorrow, frustration, remorse, or fear may express the emotion as anger.

Responding to Violence Internally

Understanding Fear

The best way to prepare for a violent situation is to understand fear. Fear is not bad. Fear is an internal judgment that something is wrong. It instructs us to be cautious. Not understanding fear, or denying it, is dangerous. Sooner or later we will experience a situation that creates fear in us. If we are not prepared for the fear, it can be overwhelming, perhaps just when we most need to be thinking clearly.

Love As Antidote to Violence

Love is the best remedy for the impulse to violence inside of us and for the fear of violence from outside. The Bible brings together the concepts of fear, love, and our position as God's children in a beautiful, intertwining circle. When we are secure in awareness of being held in the very heart of God, we have confidence to go into danger if necessary. We can enter dangerous situations not because we are invulnerable, but because we know that God, who sees the big picture, has more concern for us than we can have even for ourselves.

The familiar words in 1 John 4:18 remind us, "There is no fear in love, but perfect love casts out fear." The rest of the chapter tells us how. The focus is on our relationship as beloved children of God. In verse 16 we are told that God is love, and when we live in love we live in God, because God lives in us. Verses 7-10 reveal God's love toward us, shown by sending Jesus as a nonviolent response to a violent world. We are encouraged to follow this example, thus becoming like God. In 2 Timothy 1:7 we read that God has not given us a spirit of fear. Instead we have available to us the Spirit of power, love, and a sound mind (KJV).

Romans 8:15 brings it all full circle, telling us we have not been given a spirit of fear as slaves but have been made children of God, children so secure in our relationship that we call him "Father God." A beautiful connection is made in Matthew 5:43-46, as Jesus speaks about loving even our enemies. After instructing his listeners to love even those who do violence to them, he tells them this is a way of strengthening their relationship to God who sends rain on everyone, even those who are evil. Fear is vanquished by accepting the love of God which makes us God's children. By exercising that love, even toward our enemies, we step into our heritage and expose the cycle of fear and violence.

Valuing Full Living

Risking Our Lives

My brother once stopped to help a man whose car had broken down by the road. While thanking him, the traveler said, "What are you, Mennonite or Amish? Those are the only people who will stop anymore." Some time ago, I told this story to my young daughter who asked why more people don't stop to help. I explained that sometimes stopping can be dangerous and people don't want to risk their lives. She asked in puzzlement, "If soldiers go risk their lives to kill people, why wouldn't we risk our lives to help people?"

Life is dangerous. Accepting this premise can be immensely freeing. No matter what we do we cannot ensure safety for ourselves and those we love, so we might as well be bold to do those things that make a difference. This is not a call for foolhardy risk taking. I am cautious when it comes to safety, but I hope that never stops me from doing what God is asking of me.

Avoiding and Defusing Violence

All of that said, there are ways to deal with a dangerous situation to help decrease risk and lead to a good outcome.

Contagious Calm

A parody of the famous Rudyard Kipling poem, "If," has a wonderful line, "If you can keep your head, while all around are losing theirs . . . perhaps you just don't understand the situation."

One way to deal with dangerous situations is to use creative denial. Whereas denial is refusing to acknowledge that a situation may be dangerous, creative denial involves acting calmly *as if* there were no danger. Remaining calm promotes clear thinking and can help lower the anxiety of the assailant.

A friend tells of getting in his van only to discover two teenage boys in the back aiming rifles at him. His first response set the tone for the encounter as he told them, "I won't hurt you." His calmness, expressed in concern for their safety, led to their turning over the guns and sharing with him their dilemma. Anxiety and anger are contagious, but so is tranquility.

Disarming Confidence

Jere

One evening, the staff were called to help deal with an emergency in another area. I arrived to find a hallway full of staff restraining angry teenagers. I don't remember moving down the hall, past the knots of humanity littering the floor, to stand between the chaos and a young man holding a wooden dagger. Jere was yelling threats to use the weapon if staff did not release his friends. His best friend, on the floor behind me, was yelling for Jere to attack.

For twenty minutes we faced off. Time stood still as we looked at each other, sometimes exchanging a sentence or two, sometimes standing in silence.

The breakthrough came when he was asked to think about what he was doing to himself by leading a riot. "You don't care about me," he yelled, "You just want me to do what you want."

At that moment I remembered one of the few times I had interacted with him. He had been with a group playing basketball in the gym and had been hit by the ball. I had brought him aside to clean off the blood and take him for first aid.

When I reminded him of this, he looked abashed, then relieved. All he wanted was an excuse to end the standoff, and I had just handed it to him. Now he listened intently as I reminded him of how well he had been doing and how well he would do again. In a few minutes the dagger dropped to the floor and the danger had passed.

The quality I displayed was confidence that all would be well. Confidence is disarming. A person holding a weapon is usually not in a safe frame of mind and expects the person at the other end to feel even less safe. Being met by gentle assurance that the situation will be resolved safely can come as an astonishing relief. It takes time for this to sink in and for the scared assailant to trust that it could be true. Ability to sustain an atmosphere of peacefulness is essential in coping with situations across the violence spectrum.

Conclusion

Not every dangerous situation is clearly defined. Not every outburst ends well. Not every assailant is willing to be cajoled or to trust. Yet every encounter, at every level of violence, is overseen by God, who embraces us at all times. Knowing this allows us to live life fearlessly, fully, calmly, confidently, and lovingly, even in a violent world.

Discussion Questions

1. In what ways have you experienced violence from others? Were there encounters you didn't experience as forceful at the time? What made them hard to recognize as violence?

2. In what ways do you struggle with violence inside yourself? Might encounters with you cause anyone to be afraid of you and your potential for violence?

3. Think of a time you were in a violent situation. What feelings did you have?

4. Whose story reminded you most of people in your life? Which reminded you most of yourself?

5. What do you do to avoid or defuse a violent situation?

6. Do you agree love is the best remedy for the impulse to violence inside us and for the fear of violence outside us? Why?

10

Forgiveness and Healing in Conflict

John H. Powell

*John Powell, Buffalo, New York, is director of Evangelism and Church Develop-
ment, Mennonite Board of Missions. In 1974 he left the Mennonite Church
after losing his staff position through denominational restructuring. After a
twenty-year absence, he reinvolved himself with the church through relationships with staff from the Mennonite Board of Missions and Mennonite Conciliation Service. He now works to bring other alienated colleagues back into
renewed relationships with the church. John grew up in Alabama and attended
Tuskegee Institute, where he became active in the civil rights movement in the
early 1960s. His involvements in the experiential side of forgiveness come out
of his encounters with conflict in the church as well as in the mental health
field, with which he has been involved as a longtime advocate for persons
labeled mentally ill. He is particularly concerned to apply skills and principles
gained doing advocacy work.*

My Journey

I was appointed Executive Secretary of the Minority Ministries
Council in 1969. The Council was the representative arm of the de-
nomination for persons of color. I became the first person of color in a
Mennonite Church denomination-level position. The Council was
formed at a time of racial turmoil and as diverse racial and nonethnic
Mennonite groups in the church sought self-determination.

My entry into this racial conflict arena also began in 1969, when I
made a statement to the Mennonite Church about how to respond to
the Black Manifesto, a national call for racial reparations. My suggestion was that Mennonites should empower the "minority" communities they were working in, so these congregations could effect changes
in the lives of people around them. The response was not what I

hoped for. Rather than others embracing the direction I suggested, I felt misunderstood and "marked" for isolation.

I was dismissed from my leadership position in 1974 when the Minority Ministries Council was integrated into other denominational structures. Later, disillusioned and angry, I left the church altogether. I had lost much of my faith in my environment and the people with whom I had worked. I vowed not to return.

From 1974-1992, I was in a "desert experience"—a time of self-evaluation. Why was I misunderstood? If I was doing God's work, why couldn't others understand and respond in a reconciling way? In 1993, after much struggle, I was ready to re-enter the Mennonite Church with a new sense of direction and purpose as well as a clearer understanding of who I was and how I must respond to conflict.

Conflict and Alienation

We exist in a volatile, fast-moving society in which people experience life in radically diverse ways. Information moves at lightning speed on the information superhighway. This fluidity extends to relationships. People move freely from one relationship to another; attitudes about relationships are often cavalier. We become easily dislocated from community and each other. This creates conflict and alienation.

Even as it provides instant and simultaneous modes of interaction, a fluid context leaves voids in personal relationships which only intensify conflict. Lessened face-to-face interaction leads to relationships that are less structured and often chaotic. We become less sensitive to feelings of others. We move farther apart and may be unwilling to seek reconciliation with those with whom we are having difficulties. We are a society searching to be grounded but don't know how to accomplish it. Truly we are a people in need of healing.

This world of chaos, conflict, and alienation is the one into which we are called. As Christians, we are given a mandate to be reconcilers (2 Cor. 5:18). Yet it is difficult to be a reconciler if we find ourselves in the same condition as the rest of the world. As described above, the conflict I experienced in the Mennonite Church led to separation. I felt the personal pain of being outside of the Mennonite community. My relationship with the church needed healing.

To effect change in my relationship with others, I learned I must first pursue my own healing. This internal healing process can lead us into right relationship with first ourselves and then others.

The Healing Process

All of us are creatures on a journey through our environment—present and past. Our experiences determine how we respond to others. When we enter a relationship, we bring our "baggage" from the past. We encounter others who likewise bring their experiences. Both parties respond to the same situation with their own expectations and points of reference. Such differences can lead to conflict. Healing is the often difficult process in which we come to peace with our own baggage and the baggage that others bring.

How Did You Get Over It?

As I move in Anabaptist circles, I have been asked in various ways, "How did you 'get over it'?" That is, how have I found myself in a position to work positively, without anger, in an environment and with people with whom I have previously been in conflict?

I have not completely "gotten over it." Like life itself, the healing process is a journey. So I am still in process. My wilderness experience helped me reflect on things that needed to occur before reconciliation was possible. I found the way to inner peace, which has led me down the road toward recovery. I suspect most of us seeking to be whole are in the same position.

Forgiveness Begins with Self-Evaluation

To begin the process of healing, we must enter a cycle of forgiveness. This cycle is continually interwoven with self, environment of conflict, and people involved in that environment. But the process must start with oneself: personal evaluation and self-healing. Then it can extend to others who are part of the conflict, providing them with an opportunity to find personal healing and forgiveness as well. The cycle doesn't stop there, however. Rather, it comes full circle again to self. Forgiveness is a continual cycle of giving and taking, understanding and accepting both self and others.

When I left the church, I was angry and disillusioned. The irony is that I made myself a prisoner with this attitude. Until something changed, I could not experience the reconciliation I longed for. Forgiveness is liberation. But where does one begin? To liberate myself, I first had to confront myself. During my time of self-evaluation, I realized part of the problem rested with me. I was brash, young, sure of right and wrong. I had all the answers. I was unable to see anyone else's position. I learned that admitting my role in the conflict opened the process of forgiveness.

A particular incident came to mind. In the heat of passion during a confrontation with a colleague, conflict escalated. The person was silenced. This colleague turned to me and responded, "Just because you have silenced me does not mean you have changed my mind."

I did not realize the significance of this until I began to confront myself and realized how I had contributed to the problem. I had to admit I brought certain expectations and self-will to this encounter. If my response had been different, my colleague's response would have been different as well. Once I acknowledged this, I was able to begin forgiving myself.

Forgiveness Is About Learning, Not Just Forgetting

Having admitted our role in conflict, it is important to forgive ourselves. There is no need to feel guilty. The past is past; guilt will not change it. How often have we heard someone say, "I can forgive myself, but I can't forget"? If we continually relive past conflict "like it happened yesterday," it may be an indication that we have not yet experienced forgiveness of self.

Whether we are in a situation of seeking to forgive ourselves or others, forgetting and remembering are both essential to the process. It is helpful to distinguish between and to define the two.

Forgetting does not mean no longer having awareness of the hurt. Rather, forgetting means not holding past trespasses against ourselves or another. In turn, *remembering* is not a regular rehashing of the past. Instead, remembering allows us to learn from the past to keep from making the same mistake again.

Self-healing requires self-acceptance. We have to be able to say, "I make mistakes and it's okay." While we cannot change the past, the future can be changed if we decide to take new actions. The first such action involves learning from the past, not simply forgetting.

For example, conflict is often kindled by criticism. When we feel rejected by others' comments, our instinctive response is to recoil. But many times criticism of our actions may be warranted. To discover the truth about ourselves in conflict, we must accept and learn from these valid observations and must be ready to change as a result.

Acknowledging Basic Feelings and Needs

To forgive and learn from conflict requires understanding the important part feelings play in human interactions. We have often been told we should not feel certain things because such feelings are wrong. We have subscribed to an idea of "right feelings." We tend to forget we are emotional beings. In confronting myself, I learned quickly that feelings are neither wrong nor right. What may be wrong or right are actions based on those feelings.

Acknowledgment of the feelings and needs on all sides of a conflict provides another entry point for understanding and forgiving both ourselves and others. At the end of every feeling is a human being with needs who is affected by how we respond. One response triggers another accordingly. So if we respond positively and forgivingly, those with whom we have conflict will often reciprocate.

This was a hard lesson for me to learn. It is still a difficult lesson for me to put into practice. But this process does not require perfect people. In this journey, we will never arrive at perfection. All parties to conflict are needy people, striving toward some form of perfection. All are in process.

Key Needs:
Self-Worth, Belonging, Contributing

What is needed to forgive? In addition to basic needs for food, air, water, shelter, and personal safety, we all have social needs: a sense of self-worth and belonging, of being in community with others. We also need to be valued as persons in our own right, not in light of someone else. We all want to be appreciated, respected, and loved for what we bring into a relationship.

Equally important, we need to see that others with whom we share conflict are in the same state. They have similar needs and struggle with similar issues and concerns. The difference is that they are approaching the experience from their own particular set of values and circumstances.

Amid active conflict, it is often difficult to recognize others' needs. This is especially true in a society which emphasizes performance and competition. There is a desire to achieve and be the best at what has been put before us. When conflict evolves in such an environment, the person who shouts the loudest or presents the most compelling argument tends to be the winner. When competing forces are at odds with each other, "might makes right."

When we feel less powerful, our self-worth is challenged and another's worth elevated. We may no longer feel safe, valued, and connected. This makes it doubly hard to recognize the still-present need for forgiveness of self and of the other. We must remind ourselves to see the other as a fellow human being with needs like our own.

Conflict Dynamics

Inability to forgive both ourselves and others leads to isolation. Why? First, in all encounters we receive a positive response, no response, or a negative response. In cases of conflict, we typically get a negative response or none. This starts a cycle of fear and distrust, followed by paralysis or attack. We begin to lose feelings of self-worth and may become further alienated. Finally, isolation (sometimes self-imposed) occurs.

As I reflected on my own conflict experience, I discovered this was the action sequence I had followed. As I opened myself to the forgiveness process, I again had to confront my own fear. I had to feel adequate about who I am and what I want to become in order to regain a sense of self-worth. Finally, I had to relearn to appreciate the worth of others.

Out of such change grew a new sense of community in which I could be more open to others' experiences. I was able to look not at the past, but rather the present—accepting individuals for who they are and what they bring to our relationship, even when conflict occurs. Through genuine recognition that, in the words of the Quakers, "there is that of God in everyone," I began finding avenues for forgiving others.

To move from willingness to forgive others to action which is forgiving requires trust. We must be ready to believe our actions will be trusted by the other party. We must be ready as well to trust the one with whom reconciliation is wanted. Trust is key to movement toward healing and wholeness. Yet in any conflict cycle, trust is inevitably damaged.

To reconcile relationships, ways must be found to place and keep in the past what has damaged trust. As emotional beings, we tend to relive old tapes. These experiences hinder us from being open and vulnerable. It is difficult not to question whether our acts will be genuinely received. We fear that our acts will again be unacceptable. Moving beyond such defenses may require stepping out and risking. If trust is to be rebuilt, we must have faith that we will be affirmed.

We often assume that reconciliation means we immediately enter into a working relationship with the other person or resume the closeness that may have existed before the hurt. In reality, we may not even be able to walk on the same street as the other, yet we may still be reconciled. Reconciliation means that both people or parties have concurred on the need to move on. We have agreed on the terms of our relationship. We may not necessarily be friends. But in moving on, we are no longer able nor do we desire to place each other in harm's way. Reconciliation happens when we both get to the point of using the experience we have gone through as an occasion to move to another chapter in our lives. We are able to affirm one another's humanity, created in the image of God. We are at peace.

Forgiveness and Grace

Earlier I stated that forgiveness is a key, indeed a prerequisite, to healing. I also stated that forgiveness is a process of liberation. Our authority as Christians depends on our ability to forgive. If we are to be true reconcilers, we must enter into forgiveness of ourselves and others with the understanding that we have already been forgiven through the grace of our creator God. God's grace is the true focus of forgiveness. God forgives us. Because we are made in God's image, our actions should follow God's pattern.

If we are to realize healing in conflict, we must be ready to be healed. That healing process begins with ourselves. It necessitates loving and forgiving ourselves and accepting ourselves as creatures bound by habits, yet who are able to break those habits. Finally, healing means that this freedom of forgiveness must be extended to our "enemy." Our enemy just might end up being our best friend!

Having started the journey of accepting the need for God's grace, embracing that grace, and being at peace with ourselves, we begin to forgive when we acknowledge the need to see others as human beings. But how do we do so? How can we value the other? How do we extend acceptance and grace and peace to another?

When we affirm the other's feelings as valid, when we realize they are as injured by us as we by them, we walk in their shoes. We begin to forgive. Such realization and acceptance—still not necessarily meaning agreement—enable us to acquire the spirit of love for the other as a human being loved by God. When we can stand alongside the other and affirm that one's dignity, even defending it at every point, we are going the second mile asked of us by Jesus. We are forgiving. Even if we feel we do not do it very well, we try, trusting God to guide the process toward forgiveness and, hopefully, reconciliation.

Conclusion

In some ways we are like birds in a tree. Most of us birds have been wounded in some way. We have been placed in the tree for healing and well-being. But we can roam, first taking small flights, eventually soaring. At any point along the course of our healing we may fall out of the tree. Our wings may fail us.

Sometimes we are pushed out of the tree. God's watchful eye observes this and soon, or eventually, God places us back in the tree. God may place us in a different place in the tree, but we are back in the tree nonetheless. We continue to grow, to heal, and to encounter one another in and out of the tree. We are becoming liberated.

So how did I get over it? Like the birds, I am still healing. I am not complete. I continually seek to be more like my Creator. My plea to my brothers and sisters in conflict is, "Please be patient with me; God is not through with me yet." And my counsel to myself and them is, "Forgive yourself and others, and let the healing begin!"

Discussion Questions

1. In what ways do you agree and disagree with this chapter's analysis of the cycle of forgiveness and healing?

2. How does our self-worth affect our ability to heal and to forgive ourselves and others? How does fear in conflict affect our ability to forgive and be reconciled?

3. The chapter implies that we can forgive regardless of the other's involvement in the process, but reconciliation can only occur if both of us participate. Do you agree?

4. The chapter states that our enemy might become our best friend but also suggests that reconciliation may simply mean we agree on the terms of our relationship, with or without friendship. Do you agree with both understandings? Why? Why not?

5. This chapter addresses feelings and responses primarily at the level of conflict in interpersonal relationships. What larger, systemic issues of racism may be involved? Do these require a different analysis or approach?

6. Though forgiveness and reconciliation are central to our faith, we hold varied theological understandings about them. What familiar views on one or both came to mind as you read this chapter? Which have been particularly harmful or helpful to you?

POWER
IN CONFLICT
TRANSFORMATION

A TOWEL AND A BASIN. These items provide an image that is familiar to many people of faith. They are reminders of Jesus' washing the feet of his disciples and his charge to them to serve others. For Anabaptists, servanthood is a central part of the theology, it is a critical part of self-understanding, it is an attribute that brings modern Anabaptists much affirmation from broader society.

The commitment to service may also have an unintended consequence. It may inhibit talk about power since many consider power the antithesis of servanthood. Power is one of the most important but most difficult things to talk about—often as difficult as sex, race, and money. Indeed, power is often related to sex, race, and money. Power is an important part of a host of factors large and small. It is present and significant in every conflict; including parent/child, co-worker, church families, government, international relationships. Conflict cannot be dealt with effectively without talking about power.

Webster defines power as "the possession of sway or controlling influence over others; control; authority; command; government; influence; ascendancy, whether personal, social, or political."[39] More simply, power is the ability to act. Any discussion of power will be challenging because power is an incredibly complex factor. It is useful when dealing with conflict to ask how each person involved is using power. One way of categorizing use of power is power over (dominating others), power with (collaborating with others), and power to (encouraging others to use their power).

It is also critical to understand sources of power. What are the elements or characteristics that give one power? These factors vary according to society since power is largely related to societal values. For example, our society values material wealth; therefore, a person gains power by possessing resources society values. Likewise, though changes are taking place, to be white, male, and educated is to have access to sources of enormous power.

It is important to recognize that societal values which provide power may not have a direct impact in every situation. For example, while it is true that men as a group continue to have more power than women, in some families, communities, and organizations a woman may have more power than a man. Even so, this does not change the larger social power realities already mentioned.

As we seek to understand conflict and constructively transform it, we must also look at power dynamics related to roles of those in conflict. Where supervisor and supervisee are in conflict, or pastor and layperson, inherent power differences affect conflict dynamics. A supervisor has power to influence or even terminate the supervisee's position. A pastor has more power by virtue of position, access to broader church structures, and the perception of her or his calling. Power dynamics related to roles in society must be understood to deal with conflict constructively.

Efforts to resolve specific conflicts need to include commitment to work at conflict transformation at all levels. It is possible, and too frequently the case, for a specific "resolution" of conflict to harm justice in the larger system. For example, a settlement can be reached between students who are hurling racial slurs and their targets. But if that settlement "lets the school off the hook" in terms of fundamentally examining its policies and habits around race, the outcome will entrench systemic injustice.

In each conflict situation, then, it is important to ask a variety of questions. What are the sources of power of those in the conflict? Is there a substantial power imbalance? How can the less powerful become more empowered? Is power being misused or abused? What does the interpersonal conflict tell us about power and possible oppression in the broader social structures?

The following three chapters will examine several of these issues. Chapter 11 examines social power in general as well as power found in organizations. Chapter 12 focuses on race and power. Chapter 13 discusses gender and power. Each topic is complex and needs far more discussion than it has been possible to include here. There are many different opinions and perspectives on each of the issues; those presented may create tension for those who see things differently. Using the suggestions from the earlier parts of the book, hopefully any such tensions will lead to constructive dialogue and a better understanding of how to bring about lasting peace.

11

Systemic Power

Iris de Leon-Hartshorn

Born in Laredo, Texas, Iris grew up on the southern California coast. From a young age she has cared deeply about people, a trait she attributes to her father, who would do anything for anybody. As parent, minister, and woman of color, Iris is dedicated to finding ways to be faithful to the gospel. Among special commitments is intent to name abuse of power in society and in the church as sin and to suggest ways of transforming such abuse into creative and constructive uses of power. Iris is currently Peace and Justice Ministries Director for Mennonite Central Committee.

> Now the serpent was more crafty than any other wild animal that the Lord God had made. He said to the woman, "Did God say, 'You shall not eat from any tree in the garden'?" The woman said to the serpent, "We may eat of the fruit of the trees in the garden; but God said, 'You shall not eat of the fruit of the tree that is in the middle of the garden, nor shall you touch it, or you shall die.'" But the serpent said to the woman, "You will not die; for God knows that when you eat of it your eyes will be opened, and you will be like God, knowing good and evil."
>
> So when the woman saw that the tree was good for food, and that it was a delight to the eyes, and that the tree was to be wanted to make one wise, she took of its fruit and ate; and she also gave some to her husband, who was with her, and he ate. (Gen. 3:1-6)

Acknowledging the Presence of Power

Scripture and the Allure of Power

Power is a reality of life. Its existence makes a difference in human relations. Power can be used to make life better for people, and it can be oppressive. There seems to be an alluring quality about power that draws people. Stories that illustrate the human quest for power are found throughout history, beginning with Adam and Eve, tempted by the serpent to be like God. They could not resist. The desire for power is also central in the Tower of Babel story.

> Now the whole earth had one language and the same words. And as they migrated from the east, they came on a plain in the land of Shinar and settled there. And they said to one another, "Come, let us make bricks, and burn them thoroughly." And they had brick for stone, and bitumen for mortar. Then they said, "Come, let us build ourselves a city, and a tower with its top in the heavens, and let us make a name for ourselves; otherwise we shall be scattered abroad on the face of the whole earth "
> The Lord came down to see the city and the tower, which mortals had built. And the Lord said, "Look, they are one people, and they have all one language; and this is only the beginning of what they will do; nothing that they propose to do will now be impossible for them. Come, let us go down, and confuse their language there, so that they will not understand one another's speech." (Gen. 11:1-7)

Humans have long craved control. They have understood the potential power that comes with working together. They have also used power for self-preservation and self-promotion. These stories illustrate the potential that power has to lead us contrary to God's will. They show that Jesus too faced such issues, because at the beginning of Jesus' ministry, Satan dangled power before him. Jesus' response provides an interesting contrast to the above stories.

> Then Jesus was led up by the Spirit into the wilderness to be tempted by the devil. He fasted forty days and forty nights, and afterwards he was famished. The tempter came and said to him, "If you are the Son of God, command these stones to become loaves of bread." But he answered, "It is written, 'One does not live by bread alone, but by every word that comes from the mouth of God.'"
> Then the devil took him to the holy city and placed him on the pinnacle of the temple, saying to him, "If you are the Son of God, throw yourself down; for it is written, 'He will command his angels concerning you,' and 'On their hands they will bear you up, so that you will not dash your foot against a stone.'" Jesus said to him, "Again it is written, 'Do not put the Lord your God to the test.'"
> Again, the devil took him to a very high mountain and showed him all the kingdoms of the world and their splendor; and he said to him, "All these I will give you, if you will fall down and worship me." Jesus said to him, "Away with you, Satan! for it is written, 'Worship the Lord your God, and serve only him.'" (Matt. 4:1-10)

Jesus knew the dangers that accompany longing for power. In contrast to Adam and Eve and the people who built the Tower of Babel, Jesus kept power in its proper place. While power itself is not inherently bad, it frequently is used in ways that are destructive and contrary to the will of God.

Power Defined

Power encompasses freedom to delineate reality, to define what is true, to create visions of what should be, to set the limits of what is possible. The term *power* is used in many different contexts and can be understood in many different ways. We speak of the power of the Holy Spirit in a spiritual context, for example. We also talk of personal power when referring to the inner strength through which an individual overcomes difficulties.

The focus in this chapter is on systemic power, power found in cultural patterns and institutions. Systemic power exists when one group imposes its standards and norms through institutions and cultural patterns. Its way of doing things gets woven into the basic fabric of a society. The story about the Tower of Babel illustrates important aspects of systemic power, including need for control, yearning for security, and desire to promote what the group considers important.

Discomfort in Talking about Power

People often feel uncomfortable speaking about power. I feel unqualified to write about power, for example, because I know many people live under more oppressive conditions than myself. Some find power hard to talk about because they can neither see nor understand it.

Systemic power develops over time as the culture develops and systems emerge. Individuals are born into social systems with structures already in place. Those individuals who are a part of the group that developed or inherited the structures and who benefit from them feel comfortable in the system. It may, in fact, be invisible to them. If the system is pervasive enough, those who are part of the dominant group may begin to believe that the existing structure is the only reality. They may even become judgmental and consider other ways inferior, if not immoral. Talking about power to people in power amid such a system creates insecurity.

Power seems particularly difficult to discuss in Anabaptist circles due to valuing of servanthood. Servants are commonly seen as people who don't have power. As a result, a servanthood identity tends to cover up issues of power in churches and church institutions.

Systemic Power and Conflict

Abuse of Societal/Structural Power

Systemic power is the most critical type of power in society. This is the power that results in benefits for the white population in the United States and oppression for others. It is due to systemic power that norms and standards of the dominant culture become established in the agencies and churches. Societal/structural power has had a tremendously negative impact on individuals, homes, churches, and communities. As a Mexican-American woman, I have personally experienced oppressive forces that have tried to keep me from being who I am.

Forced to Give Up

At age five, when I entered school, I not only had to give up my native Spanish language but was put in a speech class to lose my accent. I remember the speech teacher getting frustrated with me because I would say the word *chair* with a "sh" sound, much as my mother says chair even today. The message given to me, and reinforced throughout my educational experience, was that I needed to speak perfect English in order not to be "stupid." Yet it seemed okay to have a French or German accent. I didn't notice children with other accents going to speech class.

In eighth grade, as I was preparing to go to high school, a high school counselor told me I shouldn't plan on going to college. I was encouraged to look into vocational training since Mexicans really weren't smart enough to make it through college. This was said even though I had a 3.8 grade point average. If my eighth-grade teacher had not spoken up in my defense, I would have followed the counselor's advice.

The systemic power that results in a comfortable system for the powerful can be oppressive to those who are not a part of the majority. Those with power don't think about their power. They don't need to. They don't have to pay attention to what is happening until a crisis occurs.

There is another side to social power that needs to be considered. What about life for those without power? What is familiar to the powerful may be strange to the powerless. Structures and patterns that benefit those who developed the system may be detrimental to those lacking opportunity to influence the system. The power the majority may not see and may even deny is obvious to those who are powerless.

The misuse of power is not only destructive to the oppressed but also to those in power. Conflict cannot be dealt with constructively and permanently if the reality of power is not acknowledged and structural power dynamics and inequities are not addressed and resolved. At best, attempts to deal with conflict without addressing systemic power will result in superficial resolutions. At worst, the conflict will intensify to the point of war.

Churches and Systemic Power

My work and special interest has focused on the use of systemic power in the Mennonite church. The same systemic power that has so permeated our society also permeates Mennonite faith communities. This can be seen in church conferences. The white dominant culture in the U.S. and Canada has set the norms and standards for how worship is done in most conference-based gatherings. Hispanic, African-American, Asian, or Native American brothers and sisters are invited to be part of the worship, but the format does not reflect their culture. An ethnic song in another language may be included, but the style of worship remains Euro-American. Why? Because such worship feels comfortable to the majority with the systemic power to control such things.

The primary strategy for achieving ethnic diversity in worship is by starting ethnic churches. The ethnic churches are free to develop a style of worship comfortable to them. Yet if the body of Christ includes every person who is part of our faith community, should not the churches and style of worship more generally reflect that?

The Relationship of Church and Society

Our People

A pastor called me some time ago about an immigration problem. He began by assuring me it didn't have to do with "those lazy Mexicans on the border who were causing all those immigration problems." I stopped him and told him I was one of those Mexicans from the border. There was silence, but I was determined I wasn't going to rescue him from his racist comments. Finally, he commented, "Well, you know what I mean."

He told me he was calling because a group of Old Colony Mennonites was in a jam. The group members had all been using false Canadian social security numbers and wanted to know what would happen to them. I told him the group would be deported. He assured me these were decent people and asked if there was anything I could do.

I thought to myself that if Mexicans had been the ones using false numbers, "decent people" wouldn't have been the label applied.

I explained there was little we could do and that Mennonites from other ethnic backgrounds were in the same situation. I told him I could give him places to call just as I had for others, but that was all I could do. Frustrated, he told me, "These are our people, people with Mennonite heritage, and we should do something more for them." I explained that all immigrant Mennonites are "our" people.

Congregations do not decide in isolation who is in and who is out. Power and resources have been used to perpetuate the white dominant culture throughout the church as in broader society. Mennonite church agencies, for example, have given money, time, and volunteers to help Old Colony Mennonites. The same resources, however, are not offered to other Mennonite immigrant groups. The reality is that Mennonite churches and institutions have primarily used their power to maintain the norms and standards of white Mennonite culture.

What to Do

How can an Anabaptist community of faith use power as God intended? There are many examples of groups using power to promote love, healing, and reconciliation. Such efforts are not without struggle because it is hard to work against patterns set from the inception of the country. Transformation is possible, however, and the church can lead the way. I suggest three ways congregations can work at transforming the misuse of societal and institutional power in their settings.

Pray

Since the misuse of power is at the core of our structures, including the church, we must view this as a spiritual problem. Congregations must be willing to unite together in prayer to strengthen their souls and prepare for the journey that lies ahead in this struggle. You can't begin a journey without adequate nourishment. Congregations can find ways to pray together in worship, in prayer vigils, with prayer partners, and in round-the-clock prayer times. When we are amid our struggle to be transformed, our strength will arise from our communal relationship with God through prayer.

Educate, Educate, Educate

Congregations must commit to educating themselves. The educational process can start with such questions as, What barriers do we put up that keep people who are different than ourselves from our churches? How have we institutionalized those barriers in our mission statement, vision and other written documents that describe our church? A few congregations are working at educating themselves through forming antiracism teams or attending workshops addressing power issues.

Accountability to the Oppressed

Finally, congregations need to find ways to be accountable to those in their communities who have been oppressed. Any work the church does in the area of power must in some way include those affected by misuse of power. This can help influence the church toward becoming a domination-free institution. Such work can be spearheaded by a reference or advisory group in the church. It is important that the work of any such group be taken seriously. It is wise for such groups to report directly to decision-making bodies. Their voices need the backing of church leaders.

Conclusion

Reconciliation between oppressed and oppressor is possible. However, it will not come without cost. In his book on the gospel of Mark, *Binding the Strong Man*, Ched Myers writes, "For Mark, the practice of domination is so deeply embedded in human history that no mere rebellion will do."[40] Myers goes on to say that the cross should serve as a reminder of the cost of discipleship. We must be willing to do what it takes to transform abuse of power into more creative uses of power that serve God.

Our ultimate hope is in understanding God's vision for diversity: "There is no longer Jew or Greek, there is no longer slave or free, there is no longer male and female; for all of you are one in Christ Jesus" (Gal. 3:28). While this passage provides an ultimate hope, the implementation must begin here and now. The challenge is to remain hopeful when the failures are so great. It is necessary to stay engaged in the day-to-day work of naming and dismantling the misuse of societal and structural power through prayer, education, and accountability to the oppressed. We must continue to work for God's reign on earth as in heaven.

Discussion Questions

1. Think of a church, agency, or institution with which you are familiar. List some of the values and the rules accepted there. Who made

them and when? How easy would it be for someone new to bring about change?

2. Power is defined in the chapter as "the ability to make the things happen that you want to happen." Do you think some groups have more power in the church than others?

3. Can you give some examples of systemic power? In what ways have you seen systemic power do harm?

4. How do you see the church reflecting the broader society? Are there differences? Explain. What *should* be different?

5. Do you think there needs to be a more equitable balance of power in the church? If so, how can it be achieved?

6. What are benefits and challenges when the powerful become accountable to those with less power?

12

Race and Power

Angel Rafael Ocasio and Tobin Miller Shearer

Angel Rafael Ocasio *graduated from Eastern Mennonite College (1987) and Seminary (1989). He was Staff Associate for Urban Peacemaking with Mennonite Conciliation Service 1997–1998. He enjoys music, movies, football, and spending time with his three children.* **Tobin Miller Shearer** *enjoys reading science fiction and wrestling with his sons. He has been known to bake a mean apple pie. He is director of the Mennonite Central Committee U.S. Racism Awareness Program and co-coordinator, with Regina Shands Stoltzfus, of Damascus Road, an intensive antiracism training process for Mennonite and Brethren in Christ congregations, conferences, colleges, and church agencies. When not educating or organizing about racism with white people like himself, Tobin can often be found running through Lancaster city's streets and alleys, sometimes even in the pouring rain.*

Getting to Another Level

Video games have not yet invaded our television set. They did, however, show up in my bedtime reading to Dylan and Zachary a few nights ago. One library book described an intrepid player's progress through a video game that included mazes, mud puddles, and monsters. After a series of interruptions from various and sundry family members, the player finally won—or so he thought. "Level two" then flashed on the screen.

More to Understand

Tobin: When I talk about systemic power in antiracism workshops, I often notice expressions like those of the player in Dylan and Zachary's story. Participants have struggled through discussions about their individual power only to discover there is more to consider. Eyes glaze over, haunches hunker, shoulders sag. What is this next ogre they now face?

Hard for Some to Face

Systemic power is power found in the system. It is different than individual power, which is power that individuals have. Businesses, organizations, denominations, even small groups have their own power. While not exclusively the case, white participants at the workshops tend to have the hardest time understanding and facing systemic power. I don't think that is by accident. Most of us who are white don't have to face the realities of systemic misuse of power by institutions in the same way people of color do on a daily basis. So we don't think about it. When we're asked to do so, eyes glaze.

Whether talking about conflict specifically or societal injustice in general, being able to identify, analyze, and respond to systemic power is essential. This is especially true in relation to race. So I'm curious, Angel, what do our readers need to know to begin analyzing the systemic power of racism?

Defining Racism

Racism versus Prejudice

Angel: It's important to understand clearly the difference between racism and prejudice. The terms are often used in a sloppy way which complicates discussions about these things. For example, I have heard persons use *racism* when talking about individual biases against another person or group. They are actually referring to *prejudice*, which is "pre-judgment" about another person or persons. While racism contains biases, it is far more than a thought, word, or action based on individual prejudgment. Racism is prejudice combined with the power systematically to impose that prejudice on another group of people.

The Role of Power

There is a second and crucial difference between racism and prejudice. Everyone in a society can think, speak, or act with prejudice toward or against others, but not everyone can be racist. Only those who have the power can be racist. Hypothetically speaking, as a Latino male, I may have negative preconceived notions about another group of people. However, neither I, nor Latinos in North America as a group, have the power systematically to impose our prejudices on another group. We cannot impose our prejudices by designating where or how others may live, go to school, or work. In North America, white people have and do impose their prejudices on people of color.

White Privilege

Another important part of racism is what can be called white privilege. An example may help illustrate how privilege works.

It's Not the Same

Some years ago I was invited to talk in a Sunday school class about racism based on my experience as a Latino born and raised in the U.S. I talked about being a boy in school made to feel that Spanish, the language of my home, was unimportant. I worked hard to learn English. During the discussion time, one gentleman said that his story and mine are similar. He explained that he grew up in a conservative Swiss-German immigrant family. In public school he was made to feel shame because of the way he dressed. This aspect of his culture was not valued by society, and he struggled to fit in.

I pointed out a difference between his experience and mine. Regardless of how hard we both work to be successful in school, society will grant him higher trust than it will give me. In a department store I may be viewed as potential shoplifter, he as potential customer. In a job interview I may need to prove how acculturated I am; likely it will be assumed he will fit in. A real estate agent may select certain neighborhoods in which to show me houses, while this man will likely have unlimited access to the market in his price range. It doesn't matter how well I speak English or how well I've mastered academic disciplines. My white Sunday school acquaintance is endowed with more trust and privilege in this society because of the color of his skin.

In the U.S. and Canada white people as a group are endowed with society's trust from birth. This privilege must be accounted for at the outset of any meaningful discussion of race and power. Tobin, what suggestions do you have about what white people do about privilege?

What Do I Do about It?

Tobin: Acknowledging privilege does not make the problem go away. People who acknowledge privilege often find themselves confused. For example, a few weeks ago I met with a group planning a large denominational gathering focusing on racism. One planning committee member identified that he anticipated most white audience members would react to a discussion of white privilege by saying, "So what? Now that I've got it, what do I do about it?"

Go beyond Shame and Guilt

The first step in dealing with racism is to understand how our systems and institutions act and who they serve. If we don't have that clarity, history has shown that we will talk past each other until we are even more firmly divided between racial enclaves.

Many white people with whom I speak identify feelings of guilt and shame when they begin to understand these privileges. As someone who has lived his whole life accustomed to the privileges afforded me as a white person, I understand such feelings. It is important to understand that identifying white privileges is not about encouraging guilt. It is about identifying what racism does: based on race, racism gives power and privilege to some and deprives others.

Go beyond Intentions

Sometimes people justify racism by focusing on their good intentions. Let me give an example.

That's Not the Way We Do It Here

I had a colleague who requested a change in transportation procedures in the organization we both worked for. While she, a Hispanic female, had carefully explained her reasons for requesting the change (arising from her cultural norms and standards), she was told, "That's not the way we do things here."

I had a subsequent conversation with the manager responsible for developing and enforcing those policies. I suggested that by refusing to change the transportation policies because that wasn't the way things were done, the white-controlled institution had ignored power inequities and engaged in overt racism. The manager said over and over again, "But we didn't intend that to be the case."

The distinction between intentions and results is particularly important when discussing racism. I do not intend to be the recipient of white privileges—but continue to receive them. An institution may not intend to design programs focused on fixing people of color yet still may do so. Those in power may not intend to keep attention away from the reality of white privilege, but that will continue to happen if change does not take place. Results count; intentions are not a viable defense.

It is difficult having the shield of intentions suddenly lifted away, especially for those who have never had to deal with results of racist actions. This awareness quickly produces a wide range of emotions, including shame, guilt, anger, despair, and defensiveness. Discussing the systemic forces of racism and white privilege *will* produce conflict. Angel, how do we apply conflict transformation principles to racism?

Race, Power, and Conflict

Angel: My impression is that many conflict transformation strategies do not adequately address the power of racism. Conflict is treated as the result of competing interests without consideration of the underlying forces that may favor one party's interest. Root causes of social and individual conflicts are too often ignored. This has particular relevance in situations involving persons of different racial backgrounds.

A personal example illustrates this.

Coworkers in Conflict

A few years ago I helped a discussion between two coworkers in conflict. One of the disputants was Anglo, the other a person of color. In this context the person of color, who felt wronged by the coworker, was uncharacteristically reticent, whereas the other party was animated and confident. Eventually the person of color capitulated to bring an end to the process, or so it seemed to me.

Lacking an understanding of systemic racism, I was unable to account for underlying power dynamics at play in this scenario. I should have considered and explored the weight of institutional trust and confidence felt by each party.

Did the person of color feel equally valued and trusted in the white institution? Did this person have a sense of confidence in the fairness of an institutionally based conflict resolution process? Were unnamed privileges bestowed on the Anglo coworker based on skin color? Would that not invariably favor the Anglo's interests and preclude a fair process and just outcome?

It's crucial to bring analysis of power and racism to the conflict transformation table in pursuit of fair process and just outcome. For individuals and organizations whose goals include justice and peace, a working analysis of power and racism is essential. Tobin, do you have practical suggestions for dealing with racism?

Making It Practical

Tobin: Yes, exchanges such as the one we're having run the danger of staying in the theoretical realm if we don't tie them to practical realities. Racism is a complex issue, but the most important place to begin is to ask the right questions. Here are questions that bring practicality to our messy complex world.

What Does Race Have to Do with It?

Ask this question every time there is conflict: "What does race have to do with the conflict?" Even when only white people are involved, racism may pit white against white in unhealthy and destructive ways. In our zeal to dismantle racism, we may end up trying to prove our commitment by bashing other white people. As one longtime antiracist organizer notes, "White people get confused. To attack racism does not mean to attack each other. We need to resist the evil but support each other whenever we can."

In interracial conflicts, we need to explore the impact of race on the conflict more intentionally. Paying attention to power, conflict styles, and white privilege is essential. Without suggesting that we get caught in a paralysis of analysis, we do need to be clear and open in naming power dynamics. Neutrality is not an option.

Who Do We Think Is Naughty and Who Nice?

One of the most powerful manifestations of racism is the ability of a white-controlled institution to define who is naughty or making trouble, uncooperative, obstinate—as well as who is nice or cooperative, a team player, friendly. Usually these terms are defined in relation to the experience of conflict in the workplace or church environment.

Identifying, challenging, and re-defining the use of these terms can be an important step toward creating space for multiple conflict styles to flourish. As Donna Bivens notes, "Racism gives white people the power to set and determine standards for what is considered appropriate behavior."[41] I constantly struggle with messages I have internalized to act nice at all costs, even when costs involve alienation and exclusion of my sisters and brothers of color. Keeping this question before us can open up space to move beyond the norms and standards that serve only white people. Angel, do you have suggestions?

Is the Agreement Just?

Angel: It is rewarding to help a process whereby parties in conflict agree on steps to resolve or end an existing conflict. However, if the process to reach that agreement fails to address underlying power issues intrinsic to the conflict, the "resolution" will leave the ingredients of injustice in place to surface again. The conflict resolution process itself may appear to be a peacemaking tool even as it masks injustice.

Racism is a justice issue. Privilege is power. Where race and conflict intersect, critical questions of power and privilege must be asked to achieve just results. Finding just solutions can be hard. Those interested in resolving conflict run the risk of settling for peace without justice.

Asking questions and discussing justice is a key part of the process and an easy place to begin. For example, an Anglo friend invited me to lunch one day to talk about an agency she worked at located in a small city with a sizable population of Hispanics and African-Americans. My friend asked for my theories regarding why people of color did not use the agency's services more frequently. This is the kind of question that needs to be asked more openly, often, and unhesitatingly.

Conclusion

There are many questions white people in institutions need to ask. Why don't people of color use our services? Why don't people of color last long in our organizations? Why don't people of color live in our neighborhoods? Why are all our children's friends white? Why are all our friends white? What can we do to change our exclusive, discriminating world? These questions become critical when white people and white-controlled organizations make themselves accountable to people of color. The search for answers that lead to meaningful transformation then becomes possible.

Discussion Questions

1. This chapter begins by emphasizing the importance of paying attention to the interpersonal and the institutional. How do the authors suggest making this practical?

2. In your most immediate setting (church, office, school, family), where do you see evidence of white privileges? How can you make the process of identifying privileges a regular and recurrent part of life in your institution?

3. Describe and discuss the difference between prejudice and racism. Why do you agree or disagree with the definitions?

4. Think of a conflict experience. Identify power differentials between parties involved. How in a similar situation might you put these power issues on the table?

5. Identify a positive behavior, then give it a negative label. Try giving a negative behavior a positive label. Can you name any behaviors, positive or negative, that institutions try to control using positive and negative labels?

13

Power, Gender, and Conflict

Elaine Enns and Ched Myers

Canadian Mennonite **Elaine Enns** *works in conflict management and restorative justice as educator, organizer, and mediator. She is Associate Director at the Center for Peacemaking and Conflict Studies, Fresno (Calif.) Pacific University. As one who works with women in typically male-dominated fields, Elaine is sensitive to the struggle for women's perspectives to be heard.* **Ched Myers** *is an ecumenical theologian, social justice activist, writer, and teacher based in Los Angeles. His most recent book is* Say to This Mountain: Mark's Story of Discipleship *(Orbis, 1996). For two decades Ched has tried to help peace and justice groups and organizations practice stated ideals of gender equality. Both Ched and Elaine believe healthy relationships between men and women are fundamental to the worldwide struggle over power and justice. They share a commitment to biblical justice on one hand and conflict transformation on the other.*

I Feel the Pain

Mary Ramerman was lay minister at a dynamic inner city Catholic church in Rochester, N.Y. Loved by the large congregation, she was deeply involved in the parish's many neighborhood programs serving the poor and marginalized. In 1993 the congregation designated her "co-pastor"; she began sharing in the Eucharistic celebration at the altar during Mass. The congregation gave her a stole to wear over her shoulder as a sign of community leadership and ministry.

In September 1998, on direct orders from the Vatican, the bishop summarily dismissed Mary because of her "quasi-priestly" activity. The parish strenuously but fruitlessly protested. Mary was told that when the new priest came she would be asked to take off her stole.

Her last sermon was entitled "Why I Will Not Remove This Stole." Throughout the sermon, she wrestled with the many ways women are devalued and humiliated in society. "When I think of being stripped of this stole that you have given me, I feel the pain of women everywhere wondering if they are valued. When I think of a male priest coming in and stripping off this stole, I feel the pain of older women trying to live off a lower Social Security check than the men in their lives. And when I think of this stole being stripped off I feel the pain of professional women being shut out of promotions and decisions. And I feel the pain of abused and humiliated women struggling to raise themselves out of the rejection of their loved ones. I feel the pain of homemakers with small children wondering if their life's work is valued by society. I feel the pain of a teenage girl frantically trying to diet, to discover the beauty that already exists in her. And I feel the pain of women in Haiti, wondering how they will feed their children every day. When you strip off the stole of women in ministry you strip away the value that God places on women."

Why Do You Make Trouble for Her?

At the beginning of Mark's Passion narrative, Jesus is gathered with his community when a somewhat mysterious woman approaches him and begins anointing his head with ointment (Mark 14:3-9). This highly symbolic act—associated in the Hebrew Bible with the prophet who designates the king[42]—annoys the male participants at the dinner, who scold her. But Jesus defends her initiative and her insight while sharply rebuking his colleagues: "Leave her alone! Why do you make trouble for her?" (14:6; translation from Greek here and elsewhere in chapter by author Meyers). This object lesson concerning female discipleship is so important that Jesus exhorts us to remember it "wherever the good news is proclaimed around the world" (14:9). Sadly, however, the church throughout its history has too often ignored this counsel and has persisted in "making trouble for women."

This was certainly true at the Rochester church, where a remarkable experiment in shared leadership was quashed to keep the priestly roles exclusively male. Such categorical exclusion of women from leadership is unfortunately not unique to the Roman Catholic tradition. Women still labor under second-class citizenship in most Protestant and Anabaptist denominations.

This chapter will first look briefly at the biblical commitment to equality, then examine three aspects of gender conflict today: equal hearing, equal opportunity, and equal respect.

The Biblical Vision of Equality

There is a long tradition of patriarchy (literally, "the rule of the fathers") in Christianity as well as society in general. Cultural patterns and assumptions about male power and privilege have often gone unchallenged and have been endorsed theologically by many churches. On the other hand, there have always been some Christian traditions that believe in biblical feminism, that women are equal to men and have rights and responsibilities to exercise gifts in all areas of church and society.

Theologically the concept of equality is grounded in creation—both men and women were created in the image of God (Genesis 1:27)—and in redemption. The salvation story is rooted in the account of the Exodus, which reveals YHWH as a God who hears the cry of the oppressed and who liberates. Throughout the Bible this God uses women as well as men to speak the truth (Tamar), to lead Israel (Miriam), to protect life (Rahab), and to interpret the Scriptures (Huldah).

Christians believe that the vision of the Exodus God is most fully realized in Jesus of Nazareth. How Jesus receives and treats women is instructive. From the beginning of the gospel story to its conclusion women are central actors. Examples range from Mary and Elizabeth (Luke 1) to the women who bear witness to the Risen Christ (Luke 24). Indeed in Mark's gospel it is the men who abandon Jesus. The women are portrayed as the true disciples who serve, follow, and accompany Jesus to the cross (Mark 15:40f).

This vision of equality was important also to the apostle Paul. In Galatians, Paul contends that the three fundamental categories of hierarchy in the ancient world have been leveled: "There is no longer Jew or Greek, slave or free, male or female, for you are all one in Christ Jesus" (Gal. 3:28). Elsewhere Paul elaborates on this notion by asserting that the goal of overturning hierarchies of power is not sameness, nor reversal of power, but rather "a question of equality. Those who had much didn't have too much; those who had little had enough" (2 Cor. 8:14-15). Here the apostle, who is citing the old story of the manna in the wilderness (Exod. 16), was trying to persuade a relatively well-off church to share material surplus with other believers who had less. However, the principle applies as well to the sharing of gender power.

Our modern thinking about power assumes that human beings (who are essentially selfish) must compete for influence and prestige in a world of scarcity and threat. This worldview generates competition rather than cooperation, anxiety rather than faith, and greed rather than sharing. The biblical view, however, as articulated in the manna story, is that God's creation is abundantly sufficient—as long as human beings live according to limits and commit themselves to sharing resources and power. Inequalities of power, then, are dictated neither by nature nor by the design of God, for the God of Exodus, Jesus, and Paul desires that all be free and that all be one.

To practice and promote the vision of equality today continues to be a challenge. Below we examine three ways conflict related to "sexism" (power inequities due to gender) shapes how men and women relate. In each case we will look briefly at an example of power imbalances, constructive responses, and what to do when change is resisted.

Backlash

When long-standing patterns are challenged, there is resistance. Change is uncomfortable. After these patterns have begun actually to change, there is another form of resistance. This latter opposition is "backlash." There is much backlash in the struggle for gender equality because all of us—women and men—must change to address patterns of sexism.

After two decades of modest changes in gender roles and behavior, interpersonal and institutional backlash is increasingly widespread. For example, assertive women are often labeled overly aggressive, demanding, or "bitchy." They may be delegitimized or even demonized. This labeling must be challenged, yet we must also refuse to allow it to escalate the conflict. Instead we must seek patiently but firmly to set aside name calling and continue to support the legitimate right of women to make themselves heard and understood. Consistent and persistent practice of these alternatives leads to new patterns and institutional cultures.

Equal Hearing

The Problem of Silencing

A string of enraging events occurred in the course of Beth's volunteer experience with a church task force. In committee meetings Beth was expected to take notes. She often felt that the opinions she offered were ignored. Once when Beth was trying to voice her opinion, the male chairperson interrupted to "clarify" her thoughts and feelings. His attempt to define Beth's reality contradicted what she was saying.

When these incidents occurred, Beth would feel tears welling. She would be so frustrated she was unable to articulate what she was thinking. It seemed her male colleagues became more assertive and aggressive as she grew more tearful. She would leave the meeting embarrassed by her emotional outbreak. Confusion and self-doubt would arise: *These are nice people; surely they wouldn't do anything to hurt me or put me down. What am I doing that is creating this terrible experience? Am I being inappropriate? How can I change myself so this doesn't happen? I need to be stronger and tougher. I need to learn how to think and act like a man. I hate it when I cry.*

These experiences made Beth question what she was thinking and feeling and silenced both her inner and spoken voices. Talking with other women, however, she began to see that although the events appeared to be random, they constituted a pattern of silencing. After months of trying to change herself, her emotions, and her reactions, Beth learned to recognize that the welling of tears and the sickness in her stomach often meant that some sort of injustice had occurred.

A common characteristic of sexism is the silencing of women's stories, perspectives, and ideas. Men and women both have responsibility to recognize, challenge, and overcome the many ways in which this happens.

Responses for Men

Men must become conscious of the dominating communication habits they have picked up in the culture and atmosphere of male privilege. Men need to learn to listen to themselves with a new sensitivity and critical ear, asking themselves such questions as—

- How often do we jump in first in discussions, establishing the "first" as well as the "last" word?
- Are we aware of when and how often we interrupt women?
- How do we unconsciously "talk over" women, correcting or shrugging off what they say?
- Are we trying to control the conversation by being condescending toward "emotional" responses and privileging "rational" ones, or by talking faster or louder?
- Do we presume to speak for women in discussions, even when they are there to speak for themselves?

To recognize such habits in oneself is a necessary step to changing sexist ways of communicating. A second step is to practice new, inclusive conversational habits in the company of other men, helping them understand the problems and openly (not silently or implicitly) supporting women's participation, whether or not they happen to be in the room.

Responses for Women

For women, the first task is to refuse to accept society's presumptions that women are less capable, too emotional, or unable to think rationally. Finding their voices means declaring these messages to be false and learning to believe that they as women are created whole and capable.

The second task for women is to refuse external patterns of silencing. Because many women feel intimidated by male-controlled airspace, forming support groups or talking circles for women can be an important step in developing stronger voices. One therapist calls this practice "listening women into speech." When in mixed company, however, women need to exercise the difficult art of assertiveness. Women can—

- Avoid self-deprecating comments;
- Insist on having a turn to speak;
- Stop a conversation at the point where we are being ignored or marginalized;
- Be persistent if feeling unheard.

Such interventions are challenging but important disciplines that empower women to move beyond feelings of victimization. They are, of course, easier if women are present to encourage and be advocates for one another.

Equal Opportunity

Token Leadership

Susan was the only woman leader in a small office suffering from the "one is enough" syndrome. She was expected to speak for women and to raise gender issues. When Susan insisted that more women leaders were needed, the reply was, "There just aren't any qualified women out there." This caused Susan to wonder if she was really exceptional—or just hired because she was a woman.

She also wondered if perhaps she was hired because she was willing to conform to the male office culture. Susan was required to participate in meetings but felt discounted in decision making. She was expected to work as a partner but was frequently criticized by male colleagues. She began to feel she could only go so far before running into a glass wall that seemed to surround her colleagues.

Susan felt she could never get inside that wall to be a full member of the leadership team.

There was a time when Mennonites and other Christians had a doctrinaire commitment to exclusively male leadership in many positions, a stance which still exists in parts of the tradition. Yet even where formal barriers have come down, the patterns often persist. Churches, agencies, or clubs in which most or all leadership positions are held by men are not configured that way due to meritocracy (men are best-qualified) or accident (it just happened). Male-dominated leadership patterns reflect ongoing sexist assumptions about men (they are naturally more suited to the job) and women (they are not interested or available).

When the gender barrier is broken, the next layer of prejudice to be confronted is that of tokenism. Tokenism is an unofficial quota system: the "representative" woman becomes a reason not to hire or appoint other women. Tokenism is often accompanied by a condescending attitude from individuals who enjoy a privileged status of toleration for the "other" (women, minorities, disabled people) rather than welcome. Tokenism is a systemic problem. It has become part of the organizational pattern of behavior and thus must be addressed systemically.

Institutional Responses

The first step in changing organizational patterns is to depersonalize the issue in the community or workplace. For example, if a woman is raising issues of sexism in a workplace, the tendency of those in power is to make it her issue. Instead, all parties should look at the overall patterns of power and responsibility in the system: How many women are on staff? What tasks do they perform? Sometimes called an "organizational audit," this gives everyone a snapshot of the actual relations of power. In most cases such audits show that women are underrepresented in terms of numbers, tasks, and pay.

An organizational strategy must then be developed. A common strategy has been affirmative action in hiring in which the whole organization sets long-term goals of diversity and representation. This takes pressure to raise the issue off existing female staff. Every time someone is hired, the overall staff balance is examined. Such strategies help change the institutional culture from tokenism to equality.

While the response to tokenism must be institutional, affirmative action has become a central 1990s target of backlash. For some it is perceived as threatening and often misrepresented as undermining "equal opportunity" by giving special rights to targeted groups. Many affirmative action programs are being eliminated.

A pastoral note is in order here. Backlash, like the initial resistance to change, arises from deep insecurities. Often those who criticize affirmative action are anxious about their own present or future job opportunities. They are frequently operating from a perception of scarcity: the more people allowed in a vocation or organization, the fewer opportunities there will be for them. We must strive to hear that pain, while reminding those who experience it of the biblical promise of abundance: if we share power justly, there will be enough opportunity for all.

Equal Respect

Sexual Harassment

A small church-based organization was directed by a popular, charismatic leader in his fifties. Complaints from women accusing him of sexual harassment and inappropriate behavior had become a pattern. The complaints were known to the all-male board but undisclosed to staff.

The director's female assistant, Barb, age thirty-five, then accused him of sexual harassment. After failing to resolve the situation in the workplace, Barb resigned. She petitioned the board for compensation for her therapy bills and lost wages. The board denied her petition and claimed she was emotionally unstable, selfish, and vindictive. Only when she threatened a lawsuit did the board agree to meet with her with the help of mediators.

In the meeting the board acknowledged that the director had a history of "problems" with inappropriate behavior toward women. They insisted, however, that he had not meant to harm Barb. They suggested that the problems may have been her fault. They could not hear her feelings of rage and betrayal. Although the meeting resolved some issues (the board agreed to annual organizational training on sexual harassment, to adopt a sexual harassment policy, and to provide modest financial compensation for her), Barb felt that the organization never accepted responsibility and that her experience of violation was never acknowledged.

This all too familiar scenario involved a combination of power factors including gender, age, and position. The board knew that the allegations were true. Despite the concessions, the board's actions protected and supported the director while isolating Barb. This served to undermine her ability to trust her own experience, making her feel increas-

ingly "crazy." The more anxious she became, the more erratic her behavior grew. The board chose to see her behavior not as symptomatic of
her trauma but as evidence that she was unreliable. Here was a classic
example of "blaming the victim."

Organizational Responses

Sexual misconduct, in its various forms, is an abuse of power with
legal as well as moral ramifications. A number of responses are needed.
First, organizations need to develop clear processes and policies to address sexual misconduct when it occurs. The victim needs a safe environment to tell the story and needs to know that a fair process will be
followed. In addition, ongoing training programs for all staff and board
members is needed.

It is crucial that churches acknowledge sexual misconduct as a violation of gender justice. Organizational integrity is built through admitting mistakes, not concealing them. The consequence of ignored misconduct is widespread destruction: polarization of the congregation; loss of
friendships; loss of faith and trust in the church; and psychological damage to victim, perpetrator, and their families. Conversely, seeking justice
in cases of abuse not only promotes healing for all involved but also
helps the group confront and change patterns of sexism in the process.

For decades there have been men who have made derogatory remarks or behaved inappropriately toward women without consequence. With the awareness in society of sexual abuse, harassment, and
other misconduct, these hurtful ways of relating to women are no longer
acceptable.

The process of finding new ways to communicate is threatening to
some. There are men who feel that they "can't say anything anymore,"
or that women are becoming hypersensitive. Some argue that if women
were not allowed into male-dominated areas of work, sexual misconduct would not be an issue. These responses are also examples of blaming the victim. The one violated becomes the scapegoat facing the bur-
den of proof. Victim blaming is a common problem in systems where
power is unevenly distributed. This is why working at gender equality,
both interpersonally and organizationally, is the best proactive solution
to problems of sexual misconduct.

Conclusion

The biblical vision is equality for all people. Perhaps nowhere is this
more challenging and important than in the relationship between men

and women. Instead of "making trouble for women," people of faith can lead the struggle to ensure that women and men receive equal hearing, equal opportunity, and equal respect.

Discussion Questions

1. This chapter suggests the goal for gender relations is equality. Do you agree or disagree? Explain why.

2. Have you noticed ways women are silenced? What suggestions do you have for both men and women to help change the way men and women communicate?

3. Do a mental organizational audit of an organization with which you are familiar. Are women equally represented? If there is an imbalance, what could be done to bring about better balance?

4. How do you think sexual harassment should be handled? When should it be dealt with openly and when should it remain discrete?

5. What reactions have you seen when someone suggests that there needs to be a better balance of males and females in leadership? What makes the discussion constructive or destructive?

6. What are the most pressing issues in relationships between men and women?

APPLICATION OF CONFLICT TRANSFORMATION

WHEN A CONFLICT IS FAR AWAY from us personally, it is much easier to understand and to solve, or so it seems. The theories seem to fit nicely. The importance of communication and the need to speak, listen, and be in dialogue seem so obvious. Respect for self, other, and God seems so basic and right. The need to take time to work on the tensions together and to be balanced in who gets their way seems appropriate and elementary. Healing and forgiveness seem so necessary and so simple when the pain is not ours. The abuse of power is so clear when others are involved.

The closer tension gets to us, the more complicated it becomes. The more personal the problems, the less clearly we can see the dynamics and issues. The nearer the conflict, the less useful the theory seems to be and the less certain we are about what to do.

The following four chapters explore conflict in a variety of contexts. Chapter 14 looks at conflict in the nuclear family. Conflict is particularly challenging here, where violence happens far more often than we care to admit, because we spend the most time together and our lives tend to be open with each other. Frequent interaction, along with constant changes that are a part of family life, produces a steady stream of tension that needs to be addressed. It is also here that we have the greatest opportunity to develop and practice peacemaking skills. This chapter looks briefly at how to deal constructively with tension in the family.

Chapters 15 and 16 explore conflict in the church. It is clear to all who are involved in a denomination and regularly attend church services that there is considerable conflict in the church. This should be no surprise when we think of the church as a family with dozens, even thousands or millions of persons interacting. Some have been disillusioned by the tensions and as a result have grown distant from the church. Others feel sad or guilty and do their best to minimize the presence of conflict. Still others blame Satan for tensions. Chapter 15 explores church conflict sources and levels, then suggests ways to learn to make conflict constructive. Chapter 16 focuses on how amid conflict to engage in constructive congregational decision making.

The final chapter in the book looks at worldwide conflict and the Mennonite response to it over the years. While international conflict often seems far away, allowing us to try to ignore it, the conflict in one part of the world has an impact on us all as members of the global village. Furthermore the great commission, which calls us to go into all the world, demands that we pay attention to events and conditions around the world. This chapter explores how we might apply practical peacemaking to the worldwide context.

14

Conflict in the Nuclear Family

Lorraine and Jim Stutzman Amstutz

Jim and Lorraine Stutzman Amstutz have been married fourteen years and are the parents of three school-age children. Jim grew up second of four boys in an Ohio farm family. Lorraine was born in the city and later lived in rural Delaware with a family of seven girls and one boy. They met while serving on the staff of the Mennonite Central Committee (Akron, Pa.) in the early 1980s. Jim is senior pastor of West Swamp Mennonite Church, Quakertown (Pa.) and enjoys working with a suburban, multigenerational congregation. Lorraine is Director of the MCC Office on Crime and Justice and co-chairs the Victim Offender Mediation Association board. Jim and Lorraine have co-led numerous retreats on peace, service, and spirituality.

Love Hurts

When Frederick Buechner was six, he greeted a grandmother with a "feast" of cold, leftover string beans. She was gracious. Later he overheard her comment how she normally doesn't eat much in the middle of the afternoon, let alone cold string beans long past their prime, but she would try. Buechner writes, "What I came to understand for the first time in my life, I suspect—why else should I remember it?—was that the people you love have two sides. . . . One is the side they love you back with, and the other is the side that, even when they do not mean to, they can sting you like a wasp."[43]

Handling Family Hurts

All of us have been stung by someone we love at one time or another. Sibling rivalry, parent-child conflict, and arguments with our spouse come with the territory of love. To love at all is to risk rejection, misunderstanding, and hurt. We will explore how we handle those inevitable hurts and stings in this chapter.

Family Hardball

Jacob and Esau provide a striking example of sibling rivalry and family conflict. As the story unfolds in Genesis 27, the younger twin, Jacob, uses disguise and deception to trick his older brother out of his father's blessing. He has already duped his brother out of his birthright for a pot of stew (25:27ff.)! We also learn that Mom and Dad play favorites. Isaac, who likes the wild game that Esau hunts, loves him best, but Rebekah loves Jacob. When Isaac eventually learns the truth of Jacob's lie, he is visibly shaken, but the blessing has already been given to Jacob. "When Esau heard his father's words, he cried out with an exceedingly great and bitter cry and said to his father, 'Bless me—me also, father!'" (v. 34). Who can blame Esau for holding a grudge against Jacob? Jacob wisely flees for his life and moves in with his uncle Laban.

Mom Liked You Best!

Siblings often accuse each other of being Mom or Dad's favorite. Indeed, most families have a real or perceived "blessed child." Despite the best efforts of parents to be fair and evenhanded in raising children, one seems to get the breaks. Older siblings see their younger brother or sister receiving privileges and opportunities denied them at the same age. "That's not fair!" they cry. Siblings compete for Mom and Dad's attention, love, and acceptance. Add to the mix the volatility of adolescent emotions, and you have the makings of a bonfire of conflict.[44]

Gone unmet or unresolved, such feelings carry over into adulthood. Sit with a troubled family when they are planning a wedding or a funeral, and you see how deep the current of conflict can run. Selling the home place, caring for an ailing parent, or reading the will brings to the surface the best and worst of family politics.

Consistent Love

So how do healthy families deal with the problem of sibling rivalry? The most critical aspect is to love children *consistently*. All children need to know Mom and Dad love them and want the best for them. Parents with more than one child quickly learn that children cannot be treated equally. What works for one has the opposite effect on the next. Just as we were patting ourselves on the back for our skilled discipline style with Solomon, along came Jordan. He responded differently to our "perfect" method; we had to adapt our discipline to fit him. Personality type, birth order position, and the emotional environment of the family all factor into the complexity of parent-child and sibling relationships.

It is important to dispel the family myth of democracy.[45] Parents and children are not equal in decision making. This does not mean that children should not be listened to nor that opinions should not be considered. Until children reach adulthood, parents have the responsibility and right to set down rules and guidelines for safe and healthy living.

It is also important to remember that children and parents are people. They are growing, changing—and make mistakes. As siblings move into adulthood, they face the challenge of relating to siblings as fellow adults. As children mature, they learn the wisdom and indeed necessity of forgiving parents. As children grow, parents must increasingly allow them to make their own decisions, even when bad decisions result.

Healing and Hope

Sometimes it takes time and distance to gain perspective. Jacob and Esau did not see each other until both had married, started families, and advanced in their careers. Jacob wrestles with the angel of God and receives the new name "Israel." Does this holy transformation change his perspective on past differences with his twin brother? The much-anticipated meeting with his brother Esau unfolds in Genesis 33. Jacob bows down seven times as he approaches his brother. Will Esau kill him or forgive him? "But Esau ran to meet him, and embraced him, and fell on his neck and kissed him, and they wept" (v. 4). What forgiveness! What transformation!

Like Seeing the Face of God

As Jacob and Esau reconcile their troubled past, Jacob insists on giving his brother gifts—perhaps they are peace offerings. Esau at first refuses, saying he has enough stuff. Gaining a brother back is gift enough. But Jacob insists, "for truly to see your face is like seeing the face of God—since you have received me with such favor. Please accept my gift that is brought to you, because God has dealt graciously with me, and because I have everything I want" (vv. 10b-11).

As people of faith we invite God to be part of every aspect of life. We invite God to walk with us in the covenant of marriage, and we ask God's blessing on our family life and relationships as well. God's generosity in Jesus Christ models the way of reconciliation and transformation of even the deepest family conflict. "For he is our peace; in his flesh he has made both groups into one and has broken down the dividing wall, that is, the hostility between us" (Eph. 2:14).

The challenge in a family is to see the face of God in our brother and our sister. As Jesus has modeled forgiveness to us, we need to be willing to forgive our parents for real or perceived favoritism felt during our growing-up years. For parents, a shift in perspective needs to take place that allows children to be embraced as adult brothers or sisters in Christ.

Forgiveness As Discovery

We all make assumptions about forgiveness. We know God forgives us freely and without our merit. That is God's grace. But we are not God and sometimes find it hard to forgive. "I just can't forgive her for what she has done!" we cry. Implied is the assumption that forgiveness is a commodity we can keep or give away. We can't bring ourselves to have the right frame of mind to forgive the one who has wronged us.

But human forgiveness is less an action we take and more something we discover.[46] When we fully grasp that God has forgiven us, forgiveness becomes a process of discovery. We discover that the power of God is already at work in our lives, transforming our own brokenness into wholeness, allowing us to let go of our bitterness and resentment. The late Henri Nouwen wrote that as God's beloved, "We are intimately loved long before our parents, teachers, spouses, children and friends loved or wounded us."[47] Only by the power of the Holy Spirit do we get past our human tendency to hang onto unresolved family conflict.

The discovery of forgiveness allows us to extend to the one who has wronged us the same grace that God has already extended to us. If we confess that nothing "will be able to separate us from the love of God in Christ Jesus our Lord" (Romans 8:39b), then we must allow God's holiness to pervade our relationships with those we love most. Pastoral counselor John Patton writes,

> I understand forgiveness between persons to be an important and essential part of God's reconciliation of us with each other. It functions, however, more as a witness that God's reconciliation has taken effect than as something we are required to do in conformity to an external standard.[48]

Packing for the Family Voyage

Laying a Foundation

When first married, we decided to commit ourselves to a year of family systems counseling.[49] During that same year we jointly took a course on marital and family therapy. Gaining experience in both the theoretical and practical application of this approach laid the groundwork for our relationship as spouses and parents. We developed a vocabulary for dealing with our differences. One real-life case study involved handling our meager finances during Jim's seminary days while Lorraine worked at the Center for Community Justice in Elkhart, Indiana. She made just enough money to pay the bills, and Jim's summer employment was just enough to cover his seminary costs.

What we discovered the hard way was that we had very different understandings of how the bills should be paid. Growing up on the farm, Jim learned that money came sporadically in chunks. When livestock or grain was sold, the bills and short-term loans were paid off in full. Lorraine grew up in the city and in a large family where the cash flow was steady but tight. She learned that you need to hedge against that unexpected emergency, so you pay a little on all the bills and set some aside for later.

Right, Wrong, or Different

Because of our systems training, we stopped the shouting long enough to tell our respective stories about money. When we named the differences, we could agree that one way was not right and the other wrong. Our ways were simply *different*. What resulted was a third way of paying the bills. And it was *our* way of taking the best of both methods and making it work for us instead of against us. We also learned how to respond to our differences instead of reacting out of instinct or habit. It's what David Augsburger calls *response-ability*,[50] or the ability to choose a new response in our relationships with loved ones.

One of our favorite Far Side[51] cartoons shows a robot couple, complete with bells and whistles, in a marriage counselor's office. She says, "The problem, as I see it, is that you both are extremely adept at pushing each other's buttons!" Indeed, our buttons get pushed often in family settings. This is because our loved ones know our every vulnerability. Simple recognition of that dynamic is often enough to take the wind out of the attempted assault to our equilibrium. Clearing the air when differences arise gives us freedom to unlock horns and move on in the relationship.

Conclusion

Paul's admonition to the early church is instructive for us: "From now on, therefore, we regard no one from a human point of view. . . . So if anyone is in Christ, there is a new creation: everything old has passed away; see, everything has become new!" (2 Cor. 5:16a-17).

Jacob and Esau were lucky enough to see the day when their past no longer determined their present or future relationship. They forgave the wrongs committed and found a way to reconcile their differences. As God's children we are beloved and forgiven. As people of faith, we are entrusted with God's ministry of reconciliation. This ministry was demonstrated and made known most fully in Jesus Christ who went to the cross for the sake of the relationship. In him we get a glimpse of the peaceable kingdom where former adversaries and natural enemies are at peace with one another. Marriage and family relationships bring out the best and the worst in us.

Thanks be to God that we are re-created in Christ and as such have the opportunity to see others, including our family, the way God sees us; beloved, whole, and forgiven.

Discussion Questions

1. Think about your own childhood. Can you recall a time that you were "stung" by a loved one? How did the experience shape your relationship with that person? (Note: This exercise may trigger dangerous memories for participants. Be invitational. Allow people to share only what they feel comfortable revealing to the group.)

2. What was the effect of birth order (firstborn, middle, youngest, only) on you or your brothers and sisters? What similarities and differences do you see between your experience and that of others?

3. What factors contributed to the forgiveness Esau offered to Jacob? Are there some things that family members may never agree on (such as religion and politics)?

4. What are implications of viewing forgiveness as a process to be discovered instead of an act to be taken?

5. What are effective ways of responding to others when our emotional buttons get pushed?

6. Have you experienced reconciliation, or do you know of families who have? How did it happen? How did it feel? What did you learn?

15

Conflict in Congregations

Richard Blackburn and David Brubaker

Richard Blackburn *is Director of Lombard Mennonite Peace Center (LMPC), an organization located in Lombard, Illinois, whose mission is "to proclaim Christ's good news, the gospel of peace and justice—and to be active in the sacred ministry of reconciliation—wherever and whenever we can." In pursuit of that mission, LMPC provides training, mediation, and consultation services to churches of all denominations in North America and beyond. LMPC also shares educational peace and justice resources with churches, schools, and other organizations.* **David Brubaker** *owns Conflict Management Services (CMS)—a mediation, consulting, and training organization based in Casa Grande, Arizona. David was Associate Director of Mennonite Conciliation Service 1986-1988 and established his private practice in 1988. CMS specializes in intervening in intra-organizational disputes, especially in religious organizations. David and spouse Martha were Mennonite Central Committee community development workers in Brazil 1982-1986 and remain interested in international and cross-cultural issues.*

Neglected Needs in the Church

A conflict which had been brewing in the recently established church was starting to boil over. Members of the minority group—who spoke a different language than the majority group that controlled the leadership of the congregation—were starting to complain about how some among them were being treated. Specifically, the minority members were angry because the needs of some of their group were being neglected by the congregation.

Rather than become defensive and try to quiet those who were disgruntled, church leaders took action to address concerns. A meeting of the entire group was held, issues were discussed, and a plan proposed. The congregation appointed seven members of the minority group to care for neglected members. The solution pleased all.

The story summarized above, found in Acts 6:1-7, records the earliest known conflict in a Christian congregation. It had all of the elements of a nasty problem. The Jerusalem church was multicultural, with both Greek-speaking and Aramaic-speaking members. The leaders, which included the disciples, were primarily from the majority Aramaic-speaking group. The concerned members of the congregation were from the minority Greek-speaking group. The problem had to do with discrimination: widows of the Greek-speaking group were being neglected in the church's daily distribution of charitable relief.

The leaders' response to these complaints offers a model for addressing church conflicts. Rather than attempting to muzzle or silence the "complainers," leaders brought all involved together, helped concerns to be dealt with openly, and facilitated a solution satisfactory to all. Interestingly, the role of "table server," developed to solve the problem, has evolved into the contemporary church office of deacon.

The Congregation As Family System

> For just as the body is one and has many members, and all the members of the body, though many, are one body, so it is with Christ. For in the one Spirit we were all baptized into one body—Jews or Greeks, slaves or free—and we were all made to drink of one Spirit. Indeed, the body does not consist of one member but of many. If the foot would say, "Because I am not a hand, I do not belong to the body," that would not make it any less a part of the body. And if the ear would say, "Because I am not an eye, I do not belong to the body," that would not make it any less a part of the body. If the whole body were an eye, where would the hearing be? If the whole body were hearing, where would the sense of smell be? But as it is, God arranged the members in the body, each one of them, as he chose. If all were a single member, where would the body be? As it is, there are many members, yet one body. (1 Cor. 12:12-20)

Congregations, like other organizations, are complex systems. They are made up of many parts that influence each other: lay members, pastor, song leader, Sunday school teachers, treasurer, worship committee, education committee, and membership committee. The behavior of one part affects the others.

Systems, including congregations, have rules. A congregation's rules may be formal, informal, or even tacit.[52] Formal rules include a congregation's constitution, bylaws, and written procedures. Informal rules are those unwritten guidelines visitors soon intuit or are helped to understand, such as who sits where and expectations around children in worship. Tacit rules, however, are neither written nor spoken. Tacit rules include dress codes, behavior norms, making certain topics taboo.

Like other systems, congregations develop patterns or habits. Although individual members come and go, congregations have a remarkable tendency to continue many of the same patterns developed and reinforced in earlier years. Like a fifty-year-old person, a congregation with a half-century of existence has generally developed well-entrenched habits. Many habits are life-giving and appropriate, such as holding a congregational picnic every summer. Others may be damaging to congregational health.

Destructive and Constructive
Responses to Conflict

Since all systems are made up of many parts interacting, conflict is unavoidable. It is normal in congregations for there to be tension between that which is established and the desire for something new. It is natural that the many parts have different needs and varying perspectives. The question is whether congregations deal with the conflict constructively or destructively.

Destructive Conflict Patterns

Destructive conflict tends to include a number of characteristics. First, the communication between the parts tends to be indirect, with people talking about others. When there is tension, the tendency is to attack other people rather than focus on issues. Congregational participants take a position and refuse to consider alternatives. Differences become a win-lose contest of wills, or attempts are made to avoid dealing with differences, usually because conflict is feared.

In churches where destructive patterns are firmly entrenched, conflict quickly brings negative responses. Factions solidify. People adopt a quick-fix mentality as they seek to force others to bend to their will.

A common response is to find a scapegoat who is seen as the cause of the problems. Pastors or individuals in the congregation can both be unfairly viewed as causes of the trouble, although those in leadership are more likely to be scapegoated.

When destructive patterns are in place, people try to change each other. If change is not forthcoming, attempts may be made to force the opposition, whether pastors or congregants, out of the church. Other responses may be to leave with bitter feelings or to stay with a disgruntled attitude.

Destructive conflict patterns can leave a lasting legacy of pain. Hurt feelings can remain for generations when a pastor or a family has been forced out of the congregation or scapegoated some other way.

Constructive Conflict Patterns

Constructive conflict patterns have some of the following characteristics. There is, first, willingness openly to face rather than avoid conflict. There is also commitment to engage in direct dialogue and avoid the destructiveness of speaking negatively about others behind closed doors. Congregations focus on problem-solving processes which seek to address the diverse needs of all parties in a creative search for win-win solutions. In the face of tension, members are able to focus on problems rather than attack people.

In churches which respond healthily to conflict instead of assigning blame, people acknowledge their own contributions to tension. If conflict has been hurtful, a healthy congregation engages in self-examination and mutual confession as a way to bring about healing and reconciliation.

Responding to Conflict in the Congregation

If another member of the church sins against you, go and point out the fault when the two of you are alone. If the member listens to you, you have regained that one. But if you are not listened to, take one or two others along with you, so that every word may be confirmed by the evidence of two or three witnesses. If the member refuses to listen to them, tell it to the church; and if the offender refuses to listen even to the church, let such a one be to you as a Gentile and a tax collector.

Truly I tell you, whatever you bind on earth will be bound in heaven, and whatever you loose on earth will be loosed in heaven. Again, truly I tell you, if two of you agree on earth about anything you ask, it will be done for you by my Father in heaven. For where two or three are gathered in my name, I am there among them."

Then Peter came and said to him, "Lord, if another member of the church sins against me, how often should I forgive? As many as seven times?" Jesus said to him, "Not seven times, but, I tell you, seventy-seven times. (Matt. 18:15-22)

Although the focus of this passage is on sin, the process also provides a useful framework for dealing with conflict. Indeed, the steps called for in the Matthew 18 process can be incorporated into church by-laws and membership covenants as a way of institutionalizing constructive conflict patterns in the congregational system. The process emphasizes three primary steps:

- Go to the other in a spirit of humility and seek negotiation through direct dialogue;
- Bring in "one or two others" to serve as neutral parties who help the disputants listen to one another and help them come to their own mediated agreement.
- Submit to the wisdom of the church, perhaps by allowing neutral parties from the conference or other judicatory structures to serve as arbitrators.

If these steps are followed routinely, most interpersonal conflicts can be resolved while the conflict remains at low intensity. Indeed, if the steps were followed faithfully, the third step would rarely be necessary. Use of the Matthew 18 model requires a congregation able to understand and trust the process because it is committed to taking Christ's teachings seriously.

Equipping the Congregation

Congregational Education

Church members cannot be expected and will usually be unable to implement the Matthew 18 process effectively if they have not learned the needed skills and strategies. For a congregation to become "conflict healthy," there must be ongoing effort to provide education in constructive conflict resolution. Such education can be integrated into new member classes and offered periodically as a part of the religious education programs for all ages. Educational enrichment can also be provided through congregational conflict transformation workshops led by experienced trainers.

Training for Leaders

Training of church leaders in systems perspectives is equally important. Edwin Friedman has identified three key areas on which leaders should focus:

- Work at offering clear self-definition;
- Stay emotionally connected with people;
- Maintain a non-anxious presence.[53]

Leaders who work at self-definition are able to articulate a positive vision while helping the congregation stay focused on its unique mission and purpose. Those who stay emotionally connected avoid the temptation to become distant from people when there is tension. Finally, leaders who function as a non-anxious presence are able to manage their own reactive tendencies, even when others in the system are being reactive toward them. If leaders can regulate their own reactivity, this can have a calming impact on the congregational system as a whole.

When leaders do not articulate vision, the congregation can tend to drift without a clear sense of mission. When leaders place distance between themselves and a congregation or cut themselves off from the church body in response to conflict, anxiety generally increases. In cases where leaders respond reactively to conflict and try to "fight fire with fire," the conflict can easily escalate into war.

Systems thinking enables leaders to understand that no one functions in isolation. Conflict cannot be blamed on one leader, a group of leaders, or individuals in the congregation. It is the result of many different parts interacting in a way that creates tension. Equally important for leaders to understand is that conflict resolution requires cooperation among the various parts of the church. Just as no one individual is responsible for conflict, no one person can bring about resolution. Unilateral decisions or drastic action, such as removing a pastor or a family, will not resolve a conflict.

A systems perspective will help leaders understand that constructive conflict resolution requires an inclusive process. There must be honest sharing of concerns, sensitive listening, mutual confession, and collaborative decision making.

Collaborative Decision Making and Conflict Prevention

Rigid and hierarchical church structures tend to invest decision-making authority in the hands of a few individuals. When major decisions are made without input of those affected, feelings of powerlessness and invalidation result. These become the seedbed for reactive, destructive behaviors which can lead to rapidly escalating conflict throughout the whole church system.

When church structures are based on a vision for sharing power and decision-making authority, however, people feel valued. Collaborative models of decision-making can enhance morale and a sense of shared ownership in the church's mission. Collaborative decision-making thus serves an important role in preventing conflict from reaching destructive levels of intensity.

Responding to Conflict

Pleasant Pastures Crisis

Members of the board of Pleasant Pastures Church had been aware for months of a brewing conflict. They had tried hard to stamp out the fires. Having heard that the board was considering hiring a female as associate pastor, one congregational group was surprised and angry. Letters went from several members to the board, demanding that the board state clearly that "women are not permitted by the Bible to serve in pastoral leadership."

Unsure what to do, the chair of the church board called a congregational meeting. He began with a hopeful prayer that God would guide the church into unity, but things went downhill. Members of the board and the pastor were personally attacked by speaker after speaker for their "willingness to violate clear scriptural teaching." Several members promoted a vote of no confidence in the board, but the chair refused to allow it. Anger escalated. After an hour and a half of verbal assault (and some modest defense from others in the congregation) the chair closed the meeting, noting, "At least we've heard your strong feelings about this."

Assessing the Conflict Intensity Level

Conflict varies considerably in its intensity. Speed Leas, well-known leader in the field of church conflict, has identified five levels of conflict in congregations.[54] The type of intervention needed in congregational conflict is related to the level of intensity.

Level one conflict is identified as "problems to solve." This is the type of conflict churches deal with on a day-to-day basis. Although real differences exist, people are able to stay focused on the problem and can address it through normal problem-solving processes. When conflict is at the first level, most churches can deal with level one conflict on their own using normal decision-making processes.

Level two conflict, "disagreement," is characterized by a higher degree of emotionality and a tendency to personalize problems. Conflict here may require a skilled facilitator who can offer face-to-face dialogue or direct discussion of feelings. Often the skills can be found in the congregation among pastors or trained lay members.

Level three conflict, the "contest," is characterized by win-lose dynamics, distortions and magnification, personal attacks, the emergence of factions, and people making threats about leaving. Trained consultants from outside the congregation may be needed to deal with conflict that has reached this level of intensity.

The fourth level of conflict is "fight-flight." Level four conflict is characterized by efforts to break the relationship; parties either leave the church or try to force others to leave. At this level, people seek to punish or humiliate others, factions become solidified, the integrity of others is challenged, and stereotypes become rigid. An intensive intervention process, facilitated by outside persons who are skilled professionals in consulting with church systems, is typically needed to address conflict at this level.

At level five, or the "intractable" level of intensity, the major objective of those in conflict is to destroy others. The issues have been lost; personalities have become the issue. Parties see themselves as part of an eternal cause; they feel free to use any means to justify their ultimate goal of defeating the "enemy." According to Leas, collaborative problem solving for conflict at this level may not be possible. It may be necessary for an outside authority, such as a denominational official or a bishop, to intervene using arbitration methods rather than collaborative ones.

Intervention Strategies

Some churches are timid about inviting outside intervention because they are ashamed that they haven't been able to deal with the conflict on their own. As with individuals who are reluctant to enter therapy, congregations often view the need to invite outside intervention as a sign of failure. Just the opposite is true. The recognition that "We're in over our heads" and that intervention is needed is actually a sign of wisdom. When conflict becomes unmanageable, to put off the decision to invite outside intervention can only lead to further destruction and alienation in the church.

A variety of roles may be assumed by those who intervene in congregational disputes. Such roles can include those of educator, coach for leaders, consultant, facilitator, and mediator. Any of these roles might be used by themselves when anxiety is at a moderate level and there is a need for short-term help. Most of the roles are used at one time or another when a church wants help amid high-intensity conflict. High intensity conflict requires a significant investment of time and involves a number of steps.

Information-Gathering Phase

The information-gathering or assessment phase is the first level of involvement for the consultant. Here the primary role of the consultant is to discern the exact nature of the dispute by gathering information from the diverse range of perspectives in the congregation. A variety of tools are typically used, including questionnaires distributed to the whole congregation, individual interviews, small-group structured dialogue sessions, and review of minutes of past meetings and other relevant church documents.

Education Phase

In most cases, there is also a need for an educational process early in the intervention. A workshop on "Conflict in the Church" open to all members can be a useful forum for preparing people to participate in the upcoming intervention phases. It also equips them to deal with conflict in more healthy ways in the future, long after the consultant is gone. Along with the broad education done for the whole congregation, an ongoing process of coaching both clergy and lay leaders to function in the most healthy ways can also reduce anxiety in the church system.

Healing Phase

After the information-gathering and education phases are completed, the consultant steps into the role of mediator or facilitator and leads the congregation through a process of healing and problem solving. The healing phase is largely accomplished through large-group structured dialogue sessions which help parties let go of past hurts and move toward forgiveness and reconciliation. To accomplish such goals, the parties are challenged to move beyond blame when talking about the hurts they've experienced and toward mutual confession.

·Problem-Solving Phase

When past hurts have been released, the church is ready to move into the problem-solving phase. Time is spent reflecting on the diversity of interests documented for each of the workable problem areas, followed by brainstorming ideas. As ideas are evaluated, using the previously documented interests as the criteria for evaluation, shared agreements are reached in a consensus-building fashion.

Closing Phase

The intervention then moves toward closure with a written report and a concluding worship event. The report summarizes the information gathered, outlines the agreements reached, and notes any recommendations the consultant may have for how the congregational system can prevent destructive conflict in the future. The closing worship service ritualizes the healing that has taken place and signals a new beginning for the congregation as it enters the future with fresh hope and renewed appreciation for God's providential care.

Special Situations

There are special situations in which the pastor is a major cause of the congregation's trauma. The most obvious may be misconduct, whether financial or sexual. In these cases, mediation is not an effective intervention between accused and accusers. Instead, a structured process is needed to investigate allegations, determine their credibility, and plan a response to the parties.

Allegations of ethical misconduct must be taken seriously and the allegations handled according to written denominational procedures. Attention will need to be given to the accused and family, accuser(s) and families, and the congregation itself. Generally, local congregations need help from denominational officials and other outside consultants when processing a case of alleged ethical misconduct.

Conclusion

No matter how poorly a congregation has dealt in the past with disagreement and conflict, new and better habits can be developed. Most important in this process is a commitment by congregations to learn and practice healthier models of conflict management. God desires healthy, thriving congregations which can truly represent Christ's kingdom on earth. As Christians, we are called to be God's instruments for peacemaking. Dealing with conflict constructively is a part of the task.

Discussion Questions

1. What are some unmet needs in your church? Are the needs creating tension? What level of conflict intensity is involved?

2. This chapter suggests that the congregation is like a family system. What similarities and differences do you see?

3. Think of conflicts in your church. Which of the conflicts were healthy and which less healthy? What made the difference?

4. Review the Matthew 18 framework. Do you think it is a good process? Where do you see problems?

5. What skills does your church need to deal with conflict more constructively?

6. Which steps in the intervention process do you see as hardest to complete?

16

Congregational Decision Making

Alastair McKay

Alastair McKay is a British Mennonite. Having decided to follow Jesus while at university, Alastair was involved for seven years with the Anglican church. His fiancée, Sue, then introduced him to Wood Green Mennonite Church in North London. Having spent most of his working life as a central government administrator, Alastair moved to working part-time with churches in January 1996, when he helped set up Bridge Builders at the London Mennonite Centre. Bridge Builders offers conflict transformation services and training for churches of all denominations. Alastair completed a masters degree in conflict transformation in 1999. Alastair finds other people's conflicts easier to work with: a greater challenge is seeking to transform conflicts with his wife, children, and family of origin.

Wood Green Mennonite Church

When Wood Green Mennonite Church in London was formed in 1976, the active participation of every member in congregational life and decision making was viewed as crucial. Consequently, the church set up its leadership structure on a voluntary and unpaid basis. By the mid-1990s, the voluntary leadership found itself struggling to meet the needs of the congregation with the little free time they had available. They became convinced of the need for someone with quality time to give to the task. This would be a major change for the congregation; it had the potential to create serious conflict. So a fifteen-month process of reaching a decision was begun.

In consultation with an outside overseer, members began by clarifying their congregation's identity and mission so they could be clear about what kind of body a pastor was being called to join.

During this period, two of the leaders met a candidate with an unusual combination of gifts, interests, and Anabaptist understanding. After an informal meeting with the candidate in which the potential for a good fit was evident, the leadership team proposed candidacy to the church. They also provided a tentative job description and a timetable for proceeding.

The recommendation created tension for a number of members reluctant to abandon the congregation's use of voluntary leaders. To resolve the tension, a variety of methods were used to elicit views. Progress was made in agreeing to a job description but not regarding the essential question of whether to seek a pastor.

To stimulate further discussion, the congregation was asked through the "human rainbow" technique (see below) to demonstrate where they stood on the issue. The spectrum made clear that there were wide and significant differences among members. One member proposed that the group form a rainbow on the theoretical idea that one of the former unpaid leaders of the church be called as a paid pastor. There was a major shift in the group, indicating wide support for the idea. It became clear that the issues of relationship and trust were central to the decision on a candidate.

To build trust and a positive sense of relationship, the congregation agreed to develop a detailed process which would allow the congregation to get to know the proposed candidate over a four-month period. This was done, and at the end of the period the church reached a unanimous decision to call the candidate.

Introduction to
Congregational Decision Making

The decision-making process can be difficult for churches because it often brings underlying disagreements to the surface. It also involves change which can act as a focus for people's anxieties. Decision making, in other words, is likely to involve conflict. Yet all churches need to change and make decisions to move forward, grow, and stay healthy.

Making decisions in the church should involve a very different process than in business or secular organizations. The church is engaged in discerning God's will for its members' common life.[55] This places church decision making firmly in the context of worship of God, which has implications for how time together is structured and thought about. Thus prayer, song, and periods of silence all deserve a place in church business meetings. As one writer has put it, there is a need for Christians to "approach church meetings with the same contrition and openness to the Spirit's leading as are appropriate in worship."[56]

An important principle of good decision making in the church is that it requires the participation of all those who will be affected by the decision. It is worth cultivating the understanding that each person is important and has a contribution to make. As Paul puts it: "The body does not consist of one member but of many. . . . If the whole body were an eye where would the hearing be? . . . The eye cannot say to the hand, 'I have no need of you'. . . On the contrary, the members of the body that seem to be weaker are indispensable" (1 Cor. 12:14-22). Of course, it is unrealistic to expect everyone to be happy with the changes and decisions that may need to be made. That is why it is worth focusing on obtaining wide support for important decisions [57]

Some Biblical Principles

One analysis of decision making in the New Testament church, focusing on Acts 10–15, suggests important biblical principles congregations can incorporate into their decision-making practices[58]:

- the need for a congregation and its leaders to interact in open fashion through public dialogue;
- prayer by all assembled, not just leaders;
- placing high value on narrative experience, that is, telling stories of how God has worked in believers' lives;
- interpretation of Scriptures in light of narrative experience;
- the necessity for opposition and debate to be carried out openly in the assembly;
- the need to communicate a decision, once reached, in a personal and pastoral manner to those affected.

Possibly the most striking aspect of the early church's record of decision making is the focus on people's narrative experience. This may offer an important clue for addressing the difficult and contentious issues facing the church today, such as participation of homosexuals in the church.

A Basic Ground Rule: Communicate

Many problems can be avoided through effective communication. Those planning and implementing the decision-making process should communicate often and fully with all interested parties throughout the process by—

- announcing meetings well in advance, with published agendas;
- offering agendas with short summaries of each item, so people

can prepare beforehand;
- circulating information in appropriate form and length. Many people will not find lengthy documents helpful and will need summaries with an oral (and ideally also visual) presentation;
- personally inviting those with reason to be interested who may nevertheless be reluctant to participate, thus letting them know their contribution is important;
- reporting quickly and fully on outcomes of individual meetings.

It will also help to understand the hidden emotional processes that affect communication, as these will impact the work of decision making in the church.[59]

Facilitating and Recording Meetings

A decision-making process is stronger if the chair or facilitator is not the same person making the proposal and so not heavily invested in the final outcome.[60] Often this means appointing someone other than the pastor or congregational chairperson. The task calls for special gifts and skills and in the more difficult situations may require a trained external facilitator or mediator. Key aspects of the role include—
- facilitating the decision-making process through the different stages;
- summarizing individual contributions and synthesizing the group's discussions;
- clarifying issues of disagreement and testing for consensus along the way;
- gate-keeping to ensure that people are not interrupted, participants get relatively equal air time, ideas are not squashed, and discussion stays focused on one issue at a time;
- confronting dysfunctional behavior by group members, preferably outside the meeting.

Another useful role to assign is that of recorder. Ideally, group discussions should be recorded in large type on newsprint. These can be posted on a wall to function as a "group memory." This frees people to listen more attentively to others in the knowledge that their own points will be fully recorded and not forgotten during the meeting.

Key Steps of the Decision-Making Process

A Painful Story

Sometimes even relatively minor decisions can have a major impact if not handled well. A painful experience for me involved becoming a member of a church. The policy of the congregation was that those coming from traditions that baptize infants should be encouraged but not required to be baptized as an adult. Coming from an Anglican church, my own preference was not to be baptized again. Having been through the membership preparation course, I asked to become a member. I made clear my position on baptism. The congregation had a month to discuss my application with me and to raise any issues of concern. A few people told me they were pleased I wanted to join the fellowship, but no one raised concerns.

At the business meeting at which the decision was to be ratified, however, a number of people said they were unhappy with my decision not to be baptized. They raised a variety of theological challenges. Given the church's public policy, I was unprepared, both theologically and emotionally, for this debate. I was deeply upset. Although the group decided to approve my membership, I went home feeling awful and thinking I wanted nothing to do with the church!

The process used to make decisions can affect people as deeply as the outcome. In this case, although there was a clearly defined process, it was not properly observed. The individual was left significantly wounded by the experience.

Churches can take steps towards developing an effective decision-making process that can help to ensure support from all the participants, even those who may have some reservation about the final decision. In general, these steps work best if everyone involved is committed to seeking God's will for the way forward, rather than being determined to get what they want. The use of worship, prayer, silence, and other congregational rituals, such as sharing of the Lord's supper, are helpful ways to frame and enhance the meetings.

Step 1: Identify the Issue

First, it is necessary to identify and describe the issue under consideration. This should be done in clear and open terms; for example, using how, what, or why questions. If possible, avoid casting the issue in either/or, yes/no terms.

If necessary, separate the different issues. Address one at a time. Take the question, "Should the youth worker be re-appointed?" Underneath this question are complex issues that may need to be explored. Individuals may answer yes or no to the question for very different reasons. It may be useful to recast the matter as "a review of the youth worker's role in our church" with three questions for discussion: What should the youth worker's role be? How does this role fit the church's current priorities? What resources are available to finance the post? Depending on answers to these questions, a number of options may emerge. A struggle may be averted between those who would have given opposite answers to the first way of framing the question.

Step 2: Establish a Process

It is important to reach early agreement on process. People are more likely to accept the congregation's decision if they agree from the beginning on *how* the matter will be processed. A process should be established for resolving the issue, using stages and procedures such as those listed in steps below. This will include agreeing on the overall time frame and key activities in it as well as the basis on which the final decision will be made. Adequate time for reflection and feedback from the congregation needs to be offered. If the issue is complex, extra time should be allowed for people to absorb what is happening and to participate in the various steps.

For big issues, it is better if a small group (preferably incorporating representatives of the range of different views on the issue) is appointed to design a suitable process. Their proposal could incorporate the following:
- restatement of the issue;
- statement of the goal of the process (what is hoped to be achieved);
- description of the process and time line (the activities which will happen and when);
- clarification of the decision rule (who will make the decision and on what basis).

In all cases, the planning group should monitor the process as it unfolds, addressing any concerns that are raised and making adjustments as needed.

Step 3: Generate Diverse Ideas and Options

Once the process is in place, it is time to generate ideas and options, welcoming opinions and options that vary from the more popular views. It is helpful to be sensitive to different thinking and communication styles since some need more time to gather thoughts and a longer time of reflection before speaking. Some of the following could be done:
- gather suggestions on filing cards during a period of silence;
- organize small-group discussions (of people with mixed views, if trust is high, or of people with similar views, if trust is low), with a clear structure for reporting back;

- plan a brainstorming session with a flip chart, reminding participants that there should be no evaluation of ideas at this stage. Everything is welcome, no matter how unrealistic it seems;
- seek ideas from other churches or groups who have faced similar issues;
- distribute a questionnaire to generate ideas, then publicize results.

Another useful activity at this stage (but probably after brainstorming) is to discuss what an ideal agreement might look like, or to draw up a list of criteria or objectives that the final agreement should ideally meet. This will prove a valuable resource for assessing choices before coming to a final decision.

Step 4: Gather Detailed Information

It is useful to spend time gathering information about the available options. Depending on the issues, this may be done in many different ways. Here are suggestions:

- commission a study group to explore specific possibilities;
- interview people with experience of the issue, possibly in open public meetings, listening to their faith stories;
- obtain expert opinions, such as from theologians, being ready to test their views;
- use resource organizations, including the conference or denomination;
- have home groups study the matter, possibly using reading materials;
- plan a sermon series that will explore the biblical or theological aspects of the issue (without using this as a means to direct a particular outcome).

Step 5: Provide Various Ways for Response

It is worth providing ways for all parties to respond openly to the different options. It is important to offer more than one avenue for views to be expressed, and particularly to provide ways for people who do not like public speaking to respond. Participants should be free to express themselves with the confidence that the group is keeping its mind open. One or more of the following may be helpful:

- a survey;
- small-group discussion;
- storytelling relevant to the issue by members of the congregation;
- trial or straw votes (not yet a definitive vote);

- panel discussion;
- session for participants to pose questions to others in an open setting.

Human Rainbow

There are several less familiar methods I particularly recommend. The first is what I call the *human rainbow*. This is sometimes known as the *conflict spectrum*. This technique gives a quick and visual insight into the range of views held by members.

To demonstrate the human rainbow, the facilitator should designate a wide floor space for the rainbow of views to be expressed. One end of the floor space should be identified for people with strong views in one direction about the issue or proposal, and the other end for those with strong views in the opposite direction. People should be invited to go and stand at that point of the spectrum that represents their thinking about the issue.

The facilitator can now do a number of things: ask people to share what they observe about the group as a whole; invite people to share with the group or to the people next to them why they stood where they did; split the rainbow into three or four groups and have them discuss why they have chosen their positions and come up with one or two questions for each of the other groups that would help others to understand their position. These questions can then be explored openly in the group.

If this approach is being used for the first time, it is helpful to try it out first by using something easy and nonthreatening like birth dates, with January at one end and December at the other.

Samoan Circle

Another tool to structure dialogue in a large group is *the Samoan circle*. In this process, one or two people are appointed to represent the views of each of the key groups in the discussion. Representatives sit in a semicircle in front of the group with two to four extra chairs. The representatives then begin to discuss the issues.

Anyone who wishes to join the discussion can take one of the empty chairs. The key ground rule is that discussion can only take place in the semicircle: no contributions are permitted from the wider observing group unless the speaker has moved to the semicircle. The Samoan circle allows large groups of people to express thoughts and feelings in a controlled and productive manner. If discussion is likely to become heated, then this process will require skilled facilitation.

Step 6: Narrow the Field of Options

A critical part of making decisions is to look for common ground and narrow the field of viable options. A flip chart or overhead projector can be helpful to assure that everyone can see and reflect on the points identified. Throughout this stage it may be useful to continue using some of the group-response methods described earlier. This is the point at which to—

- identify areas of common agreement or concern;
- eliminate options that the group agree are not viable, but keeping useable elements whenever possible;
- note which option(s) seem to have the strongest support;
- propose amendments to existing options which would address any remaining concerns, needs, or fears; or blend elements from other ideas;
- ask those who remain concerned what it would take for them to accept the proposal.

If the issue is particularly complex, it may be appropriate to undertake a time of congregational fasting and prayer before moving to a final decision. When facing difficult decisions, the Jesuits are known to have a special meeting in which negative aspects of the main option or options are voiced. A long period of silent prayer follows. Next they have a meeting, usually the next day, to consider all the positive aspects, again followed by silent prayer. A final meeting is then held in which the decision is made with a commitment to consensus.[61]

If the process has been divisive and some feel that they have somehow "lost," it may also be appropriate to hold a special service of reconciliation. Such a service may incorporate the sharing of the Lord's supper to affirm the unity of the congregation in the body of Christ.

Step 7: Make and Implement the Decision

After information has been gathered and discussion has taken place, a decision will need to be made. The rules for making the decision should have been agreed to when the process was established. It may be useful to agree to a review of the decision after a period of time. As the time for making a decision approaches, it is good again to put the process in the broader context of discerning God's will . There are a number of ways to make the actual decision in a congregational setting.

Consensus Based on Mutual Consent

Consensus is not unanimity (an unrealistic goal in most situations). Rather, it is the readiness of all to live with a decision. Consensus requires the full consent of all present for the decision to proceed. Those who do not like a proposal can still give their consent if willing to lay aside their concerns for the sake of the group. However, they are more likely to do so if their concerns have been properly heard and the proposal modified in some way to address their views. Such agreement to cooperate is evidence of the Holy Spirit at work. In a pure consensus model, individuals can block a decision if unwilling to stand aside.

Modified Consensus

Pure consensus can be an impractical ideal. Sometimes individuals hold deep convictions and feel morally obligated to stop the congregation's direction when operating in a consensus model. Occasionally some abuse the power consensus gives them, or their own inner struggles stop them from respecting the group as a whole.

In a modified consensus model, every effort is made to come to a consensus decision. If the group gets really stuck, it can proceed on the basis of a significant majority (e.g., eighty percent). This allows a congregation to proceed after working hard to address the concerns of the minority, without having to be paralyzed by their concerns. It also allows conscientious individuals to preserve their deep convictions without feeling responsible for the outcome. This can be a good approach for churches.

A Vote By Agreed Percentage Majority

Voting makes the decision on the simple basis of a given majority. The higher the percentage, the stronger the decision will be. For most important decisions it will therefore be unwise to act on the basis of a simple majority, and a two-thirds majority is likely to be the minimum satisfactory. If voting is the approach a congregation uses, it may be worth specifying different percentages for different kinds of decisions. For example, choosing a new pastor might require an eighty percent majority, while choosing a new songbook might only require a sixty percent majority. As voting generally creates winners and losers, this approach may not be best with important decisions, other than as a last resort.

If the overall process has been well managed, making the decision often proves the easiest step. Once the decision is reached, it is particularly important to find ways to build bridges with those who do not like the decision. Do not allow bitterness to fester. As well as formally acknowledging the minority opinion in minutes or records, perhaps seek a way for their concerns to remain visible to the church. Look for ways to celebrate community life, recognize the work that has gone into the decision making, acknowledge and show genuine respect for differences, and of course ensure that the decision is implemented.

Step 8: Review the Decision

It is helpful in congregational decision making to understand that the process does not end once a decision is made. The final stage is to review the decision after time has passed. This is particularly helpful when there are different opinions about what should be done. Questions to consider when reviewing a decision might include—

- Does the decision still serve the needs of the church?
- Has the congregation moved on in significant ways that might require the decision to be re-visited?

Conclusion

An effective decision-making process which aims to include all takes time. But this investment will reap rewards later. A rushed process that leaves people unhappy or marginalized may sow seeds of destructiveness which will bear bad fruit later on. Choose the better way![62]

Discussion Questions

1. What experiences have you had of being excluded from important decisions in the church? What impact did these have on you?

2. In what ways does your congregation give space for listening to stories of how God has worked in people's lives, in the context of making decisions? How could this space be increased?

3. Does your congregation appoint a facilitator and a newsprint recorder at business meetings? How could their use be maximized?

4. Explore your experiences of the process your congregation uses for making major decisions. How does this process match up to the key steps outlined in this chapter? What are strengths and weaknesses of your church's approach? How do people generally feel when a decision is made with which they disagree?

5. How does your congregation work with those holding minority opinions, both before and after decisions are made? How could the congregation better ensure that those opinions are heard and respected?

6. Does your congregation decide by consensus, modified consensus, or voting? Consider forming a small , time-limited task force of diverse people to evaluate pros and cons of your approach and ways to improve it.

17

Global Conflict

by Gerald Shenk

Gerald Shenk worked for nine years as student and teacher in the lands of the former Yugoslavia between 1977 and 1989. With his wife Sara, he shared the life of small evangelical communities in the Balkans. Having studied extensively under Mennonites, Methodists, and Marxists, he turned to the sociology of religion for doctoral work at Northwestern University. He then returned to Croatia to teach at the Evangelical Theological Seminary (in Osijek). Now teaching at Eastern Mennonite Seminary, Harrisonburg, Virginia, he has made brief return visits for intensive teaching in Croatia each year, along with support for peacemakers across the Balkan region. Gerald and Sara have three children; the first was born in Zagreb, Croatia.

Mira

"You Americans have no idea how terrible war is," my traveling companion from Yugoslavia thundered. "You'll never understand war until it ravages your own territories. Then you will know why we are bigger opponents to war than you are, even if you call yourselves pacifists! We know what war is like and will never let it happen here again." Mira had known the tragedies of World War II, which had included atrocities and genocide in that very region.

Her vehemence startled me as we traveled together through the Yugoslav countryside by noisy train. I had been listening carefully to her anguished lament over the costs of war. I had thought my sympathetic response would meet with approval; surely she would resonate and approve when I described my people's opposition to war.

That was two decades ago. I still hear those words and feel the anguish. But I am also troubled by the fact that those tracks have been torn up and those communities destroyed again by the 1991-1995 warfare. I sometimes wonder where Mira is now.

Living in a Troubled World

"We are people of God's peace, as a new creation," we sing in the words from Menno Simons.[63] We believe that the power of God is especially available to persons who seek reconciliation and forgiveness after sin and wickedness have wrought destruction in the human community. Such a confidence should take us a long way into encounters with persons at the broken edges of our world, victims of war and strife. There is some truly good news here, and many of us have responded with a sense of calling to the task of proclaiming it in troubled situations around the globe. But what do we know about war?

A Brief Overview of
Mennonite Peacemaking Efforts

Mennonites today, claiming the 500-year heritage of the Reformation Anabaptists as witnesses for peace, have a special calling to stand together with victims of enmity and injustice wherever they may be. The question of what to do with our commitment to peace has changed considerably over the centuries. This is especially true in the twentieth century, as is shown by Leo Driedger & Donald Kraybill in the book *Mennonite Peacemaking: From Quietism to Activism.*[64]

Passive Resistance to War

Passive resistance to war has been one way of demonstrating a commitment to peace. This was the primary approach used during the early part of the century. At first, particularly during World War I, Mennonites simply refused to serve in the military. This passive resistance toward complicity in war taught us that it is possible for a small and unpopular minority to avoid participation in the militarist fever. The next generation brought us the crucial understanding of creative alternatives to war, with an energetic band of new leaders during World War II who plunged into constructive engagements instead. Programs such as Civilian Public Service allowed conscripts to work in hospitals, forestry, and construction brigades rather than direct military service.

A Vision for Purposeful Engagement

The passive resistance approach shifted to a vision for purposeful engagement in the world following World War II. This change was fueled in part by the experience of Mennonites who participated during the 1940s and 1950s in Europe's recovery projects from the devastation brought about by war. The experience of recovery and the healing of nations led the Mennonite emissaries to see that a commitment to peace could go beyond passive resistance to war. It was possible to be engaged in the world and to actively participate in recovery and healing. This vision encouraged Mennonite individuals and organizations to be purposefully engaged with the world.

Nonviolent Protest and Prevention

The painful experience of the Vietnam War moved a later generation into nonviolent protest and active resistance to war. More recent programs attempt to prevent the downward destructive spirals of mistrust, fear, and hatred that lead to war, and to help bring reconciliation where conflict exists. Now we feel positively called to build the bridges for reconciliation before and during the conflicts that wreck our world, not merely waiting to mop up afterwards. Sensing the buildup of tensions, today we send our emissaries toward the troubles on the rise, seeking understandings that may help to prevent the worst scenarios.[65]

Being Reconcilers in a World of Conflicts

What Difference Can We Make?

The vision for peace is nothing less than a direct confrontation with the powers of evil in our world. Many Mennonites have found a sense of renewal and purpose in these positive engagements for peace. What does it really take to sustain such a wild hope? Like certain biblical characters, we are likely to point out that we are only a tiny tribe among all the peoples of this world. Despite a flurry of attention from time to time, our impact will not amount to much if measured only in front-page headlines or coverage on CNN. It makes a good story when simple folk turn up several states away from home to clean up after a tornado, perhaps. And we made a bit of a splash several years ago with a determined effort to rebuild southern African-American churches destroyed in a spate of racist arson attacks.[66]

Taken alone, however, most of our efforts would appear to an observer to involve minor contributions to the larger picture. If we had to do the whole project ourselves, turning against the tides of war would indeed be a lonely and foolhardy mission. The number of hot spots capable of escalating to full-fledged warfare in our world hovers near fifty in recent years. The Los Angeles Times described the "most consistently troubling" of these as "the tribal hatreds that divide humankind by race, faith, and nationality." So why would we Mennonites imagine ourselves as part of the solution and not just part of the problem?

A Global Vision

The world of the twenty-first century is filled with tribes. Joel Kotkin describes some of them as having a global reach and global vision. Like the Jews, the British, the Japanese, the Chinese, and the Indians,[67] our peacemaking tribe would have to have a strong identity, mutual dependence, global dispersion, mutual trust, and a passion for knowledge and the values of our faith. The core of our families and communities becomes the structure for relating to the entire human family. We will be a diaspora people of conviction for building peace, together with persons of goodwill in the other tribes we encounter. Together we build a "culture for peace," and the cause becomes wholistic and constructive.

Second, we need to listen to and identify with those who suffer. Our willing embrace of suffering, rather than agreeing to cause harm to others, unites us with those who are under yokes of oppression. Because of our Anabaptist legacy of persecution and suffering, we can testify that these convictions for peace are costly. The memory of our own suffering, the sensitivity to those who suffer around the world, and the conviction we bring for peace could be just what is needed in our world today.

What It Will Take

Homework

What will it take for us to contribute to transforming global conflict? First, it requires that we identify our own violent patterns. We must do so humbly, contritely, and honestly. We must also develop a readiness to listen to, learn from, and be willing partners with people in places of conflict. As we go into the world, we must remember that all justice struggles are somehow connected. We will have little integrity in other places if we ignore the conflict in our midst.

Prayer and Communication

Identification with persons who suffer comes with a steep current price. Peace workers must be sustained with unflagging zeal in prayer support and frequent communication. We cannot regard them as lonely or impossible heroes. They are any and all of us, embodying a strange confidence that ordinary members of our communion will exhibit the same consistent response, trained and disciplined in the love of Jesus.

Develop the Best Conflict Transformation Skills

We must bring the best skills possible to tasks of cross-cultural communication and language-learning in particular. We will invest time in understanding peoples and places that seem obscure, long before they crop up in the focus of world attention. Preventive measures include vigorous assessment of long-term prospects for strife in remote areas of the human community, as well as clear strategies for prompt responses when hostilities reach a boiling point.

Listen to Frontline Workers

It will be important to find systematic ways of listening in on the agonies experienced by our frontline workers in their confrontations with evil powers in our world. Moving toward the troubles means taking on some of the most toxic waste sites we know. We must also pay special and caring attention to the wounds of our healers.

Christ-Centered Renewal

This curious tribe will need to be quite clear about our need for constant renewal of our staying power, centered in Jesus, the healer of our every ill. No member sent into the fray with powers of darkness anywhere on this shadowed planet should venture forth without such protection. I have just returned from another journey that included listening and support for peacemaker efforts related to strife in former Yugoslav lands. Asking each of our workers and their associates what it takes to sustain them over the long haul, I was struck with the consistency of their answers: a strong supportive community gathered in fervent prayer. Forms of community back home take care of sending workers and supporting them; forms of community must also be sought on location, with like-minded colleagues who share core commitments to peace. And prayer, backed up by e-mail and other diligent communication, forges the unity they need to continue their tasks.

Our Strength

The Mennonite "tribe" builds on an expanding legacy of presence and access in many parts of the globe, with some respectful recognition for the courage of our costly peace convictions. These can never be reduced to technique alone or to particular dispute-handling preferences. Our witness grows from faith, from understandings of sin and redemption turned inside-out for the sake of the world. We enact the parables and the witness of Jesus, urging and arguing that there is surely a better way, a path that affirms life and refutes the powers of death.

Our people care deeply for the victims of oppression and injustice. We have already cultivated a presence that communicates in more ways than we might imagine. Compassion ministries compel us to try to understand the toughest situations from the inside, in partnership with insiders who have come to trust us because they know we have also walked with others. Our workers come equipped to make a tangible statement of presence even though the risks are high, and of compassion designed to touch the deepest needs of the suffering human spirit.

By rooting our witness in faith, we convey a clear confidence that we will find God's people already present among other tribes, also working for God's peace. Making the spiritual connections, we show that we are not alone. Our Lord has many people in the teeming cosmopolitan multitudes. We expect to find kindred spirits and encourage each other.

Conclusion

We can celebrate a heritage of faithful peoplehood that allows us to rejoice in specific memories when we sing, "We are people of God's peace, in the new creation."[68] We can be grateful for generations of ancestors who managed to avoid war. We can be inspired by more recent generations who have moved against the violence, cleaning up the aftermath of this century's enormous clashes. We can support and participate in the most recent efforts to prevent war and bring about reconciliation.

This indeed fits well with ongoing themes in our ongoing argument as a faith community, set against the stream of the larger society around us. Our witness as peacemakers is intended to convey a sturdy confidence that the gospel of Christ has the power to change lives, as our evangelical Christian friends would easily agree. We also insist that changed lives can lead to a new community, even a changed society, as more ecumenical colleagues might concur. If there is a blessing for peacemakers, we want to have a full share in it!

Discussion Questions

1. Name current global conflicts. How much attention do you give to international matters? Are you comfortable or uncomfortable with your own awareness of or response to conflicts around the world?

2. What connection do you see between the conflicts in North America and the rest of the world? Are they unrelated or related?

3. Of the different approaches Mennonites have taken to peacemaking in the twentieth century, with which are you more comfortable? Uncomfortable? Explain.

4. Do you think we can make a difference in world conflict? Why or why not?

5. This chapter suggests the Mennonite history of suffering can be used to help us connect with others who are suffering. Do you agree? Why?

6. Which of the required peacemaking ingredients strikes you as most critical? Least important? Would you suggest others?

Notes

Note to Introduction

1. Stanley Hauerwas, *The Peaceable Kingdom* (Notre Dame, Ind.: University of Notre Dame Press, 1983), 26. See also Don E. Eberly, ed., *The Content of America's Character Recovering Civic Virtue* (Lanham, Md.: Madison Books, 1995), 171, who suggests using stories rather than "moral dilemma" case studies to build a meaningful moral tradition.

Notes to Chapters 1-17

1. Joyce L. Hocker and William W. Wilmot, *Interpersonal Conflict*, 4th ed. (Madison, Wis.: William C. Brown Communication, 1978, 1995), 21.

2. John Paul Lederach, "Understanding Conflict: The Experience, Structure and Dynamics," in *Mediation and Facilitation Manual: Foundations and Skills for Constructive Conflict Transformation*, 3d. ed., ed. Jim Stutzman and Carolyn Schrock-Shenk (Akron, Pa.: Mennonite Conciliation Service, 1995), 44-45.

3. M. Scott Peck, *The Road Less Traveled: A New Psychology of Love* (New York: Simon and Schuster, 1978), 15.

4. Credit for this idea goes to John Paul Lederach.

5. John Paul Lederach, "'Revolutionaries' and 'Resolutionaries': In Pursuit of Dialogue," in Stutzman and Schrock-Shenk, 50-52.

6. Robert A. Baruch Bush and Joseph P. Folger, *The Promise of Mediation: Responding to Conflict Through Empowerment and Recognition* (San Francisco: Jossey-Bass Publishers, 1994), 84-89.

7. This section follows Miroslav Volf, *Exclusion and Embrace: A Theological Exploration of Identity, Otherness, and Reconciliation* (Nashville, Tenn.: Abingdon Press, 1996), especially his second and third chapters. Quote at end of last paragraph, p. 42, comes from p. 16.

8. John Paul Lederach, *Preparing for Peace: Conflict Transformation Across Cultures* (Syracuse, N.Y.: Syracuse University Press, 1995), 17-19.

9. Stanley Hauerwas, "The Church's One Foundation is Jesus Christ Her Lord; Or, in a World Without Foundations: All We Have is the Church," in *Theology Without Foundations: Religious Practice and the Future of Theological Truth*, ed. Nancy Murphy, Mark Nation, and Stanley Hauerwas (Nashville:

Abingdon Press, 1994), 157.

10. Richard J. Mouw, *Uncommon Decency· Christian Civility in an Uncivil World* (Downers Grove, Ill.: InterVarsity Press, 1992). See especially Chapter 13.

11. Sue Bender, *Everyday Sacred· A Woman's Journey Home* (San Francisco: Harper Collins, 1995), 15-16.

12. Ronald B. Adler, *Interplay: The Process of Interpersonal Communication*, 5th ed. (Fort Worth: Harcourt Brace Jovanovich College Publishers, 1992), 222.

13. David Augsburger, *Caring Enough to Hear and Be Heard* (Scottdale, Pa.: Herald Press, 1982), 12.

14. Mary Rose O'Reilley, "Deep Listening: An Experimental Friendship," *Weavings* (May/June 1994): 21.

15. Robert Wicks quoted in Joyce Rupp Wicks, *The Cup of Our Life: A Guide for Spiritual Growth* (Notre Dame, Ind.: Ave Maria Press, 1997), 49.

16. Anthony de Mello, S.J., *A Way to God for Today With Anthony de Mello, S.J.* (Allen, Tex.: Tabor Pub, 1992), tape 1 of 6.

17. Sue Monk Kidd, *When the Heart Waits: Spiritual Direction for Life's Sacred Questions* (San Francisco: Harper & Row, 1992). Many books have been written on this topic. I found this one helpful.

18. G. M. Goldhaber quoted in Adler, 215-216.

19. Carolyn Schrock-Shenk, "Centered Communication—Listening," in Stutzman and Schrock-Shenk, 110.

20. Augsburger, *Caring Enough to Hear and Be Heard*, 29.

21. O'Reilley, *Weavings*, 25.

22. Susan Classen, *Vultures and Butterflies: Living the Contradictions* (Scottdale, Pa.: Herald Press, 1992), 90.

23. Ron Kraybill, "Centered Communicaton: Speaking," in Stutzman and Schrock-Shenk, 109.

24. Kathleen Norris, *The Cloister Walk* (New York: Riverhead Books, 1996), 36.

25. Kenneth C. Haugk and Ruth N. Koch, *Speaking the Truth in Love: How to Be an Assertive Christian* (St. Louis, Mo: Stephen Ministries, 1992), 145.

26. Elouise Renich Fraser, *Confessions of a Beginning Theologian* (Downers Grove, Ill.: InterVarsity Press, 1998), 116.

27. Martin Buber, *Between Man and Man* (New York: Macmillan, 1965), 99-101.

28. Lance Morrow, "To Conquer the Past," *Time* (Jan. 3, 1994), 34-37.

29. John Stewart, ed., *Bridges not Walls. A Book About Interpersonal Communication*, 3d ed. (Reading, Mass.: Addison-Wesley, 1982), 34.

30. A compilation of information from Bruce Baird-Middleton, *Robert Coles: An Intimate Biographical Interview* (Cambridge, Mass.: Harvard University Press), video; and Robert Coles, *The Story of Ruby Bridges* (New York: Scholastic Inc., 1995).

31. Martin Luther King Jr., *Strength to Love* (Philadephia: Fortress, 1963), 9-16.

32. Mouw, 9-18.

33. Mohandas K. Gandhi, *An Autobiography: The Story of My Experiments with Truth*, trans. Mahadev Desai (Boston: Beacon, 1957), 103, 437.

34. Nelson Mandela, *Long Walk to Freedom: The Autobiography of Nelson Mandela* (Boston: Little, Brown and Company, 1994), 10.

35. Stephen Mitchell, *Genesis: A New Translation of the Classic Biblical Stories* (New York: Harper Collins, 1996), 3-22.

36. James Gilligan, *Violence: Reflections on a National Epidemic* (New York: Vintage Books, 1996), 77, 110.

37. Roger Fisher and Scott Brown, *Getting Together: Building Relationships as We Negotiate* (New York: Penguin Books, 1988), 37.

38. Reuel Howe, *The Miracle of Dialogue* (New York: Seabury Press, 1963).

39. *Webster's New International Dictionary*, 2d. unabridged ed., ed.-in-chief William Allan Neilson (Springfield, Mass.: Merrian Company Publisher, 1952).

40. Ched Myers, *Binding the Strong Man: A Political Reading of Mark's Story of Jesus* (Maryknoll, N.Y.: Orbis, 1996), 2.

41. Donna K. Bivens, "Internalized Racism: A Definition," *Women's Theological Center Newsletter* (June 1995).

42. See 1 Samuel 10:1.

43. Frederick Buechner, *The Sacred Journey* (San Francisco, Calif.: Harper & Row, 1982), 32.

44. For a redemptive view of adolescence, see Eugene Peterson, *Like Dew Your Youth: Growing up with Your Teenager* (Grand Rapids, Mich.: Eerdmans, 1994). He says, "But adolescence is a gift, God's gift, and it must not be squandered in complaints or stoic resistance. There is a strong Christian conviction, substantiated by centuries of devout thinking and faithful living, that everything given to us in our bodies and in our world is the raw material for holiness. Nature is brought to maturity by grace and only by grace. Nothing in nature—nothing in our muscles and emotions, nothing in our geography and our genes—is exempt from this activity of grace. And adolescence is not exempt" (p. 5).

45. John Rosemond, "There's Nothing 'Fair' About Sibling Treatment," *The Morning Call* (Nov. 9, 1997), E6.

46. John Patton, *Is Human Forgiveness Possible?: A Pastoral Perspective* (Nashville: Abingdon Press, 1985), 148

47. Henri J. M. Nouwen, *Life of the Beloved: Spiritual Living in a Secular World* (New York: Crossroad, 1996), 30.

48. Patton, 148.

49. David Augsburger, *Pastoral Counseling Across Cultures* (Philadelphia: Westminster Press, 1986). For an introduction to family systems theory, see chapter 6.

50. David Augsburger (Marital and Family Therapy course at Associated Mennonite Biblical Seminary, Elkhart, Ind., Fall 1995).

51. Created by Gary Larson and drawn from *The Far Side 1996 Off-the-Wall Calendar* (Copyright © 1995, FarWorks, Inc.), Monday, March 11.

52. Kenneth R. Mitchell, *Multiple Staff Ministries* (Philadelphia: Westminster Press, 1988). See especially Chapter 3.

53. Edwin Friedman, *Generation to Generation: Family Process in Church and Synagogue* (New York: Guilford Press, 1986).

54. Speed Leas, *Moving Your Church Through Conflict* (Washington, D.C.: Alban Institute, 1985), 19-22.

55. See, for example, Danny E. Morris and Charles M. Olsen, *Discerning God's Will Together: A Spiritual Practice for the Church* (Bethesda, Md.: Alban Institute, 1997).

56. Gaylord Noyce, *Church Meetings That Work* (Bethesda, Md.: Alban Institute, 1994). This is a helpful and easy book to read, although it has its weaknesses, such as a relatively uncritical embracing of Robert's Rules of Order for large church meetings.

57. The need for wide participation is even greater when a congregation is formulating a mission statement and strategic plan. A useful handbook for such a process is Roy M. Oswald and Robert E Friedriech's *Discerning Your Congregation's Future: A Strategic and Spiritual Approach* (Bethesda, Md.: Alban Institute, 1996).

58. Luke T. Johnson, *Scripture and Discernment. Decision Making in the Church* (Nashville: Abingdon Press, 1996).

59. One place to start might be Peter L. Steinke's *How Your Church Family Works. Understanding Congregations as Emotional Systems* (Bethesda, Md.: Alban Institute, 1993).

60. Michael Doyle and David Straus, *How to Make Meetings Work* (New York: Jove Press, 1982). For more information about facilitating meetings, I recommend this book.

61. Gerard Hughes, *God of Surprises* (London: Darton, Longman, and Todd, 1985).

62. This chapter is an expanded version of a short article written earlier for Administry, St. Albans, England, UK.

63. Menno Simons, "We Are People of God's Peace," trans. Esther Bergen, in *Hymnal: A Worship Book* (Elgin, Ill.: Brethren Press, 1992), Hymn #407.

64. Leo Driedger and Donald B. Kraybill, *Mennonite Peacemaking: From Quietism to Activism* (Scottdale, Pa.: Herald Press, 1994). Pages 61-80 are especially recommended.

65. Douglas Johnston and Cynthia Sampson, *Religion. The Missing Dimension of Statecraft* (Oxford: Oxford University Press, 1994). Six of the contributors acknowledged in this significant work are associated with the Peacebuilding Institute in the Conflict Transformation Program at Eastern Mennonite University.

66. "Volunteers Flow Into Rural Reconstruction; Rebuilding Alabama Church is 'the Lord's Work,'" *USA Today* (June 14-16, 1996), 1A.

67. Joel Kotkin, *Tribes: How Race, Religion and Identity Determine Success in the Global Economy* (New York: Random House, 1993).

68. Menno Simons, Hymn #407.

The Editors

Since 1992 **Carolyn Schrock-Shenk** has worked with Mennonite Central Committee U.S. She is now Director of Mennonite Conciliation Service, which focuses on issues of conflict. She is a mediator, trainer, consultant, and editor of *Conciliation Quarterly*.

Carolyn was born in Middlebury, Indiana, sixth of seven children in a family known for daring escapades and saying what they thought. It was there she learned how to play and fight competitively and passionately. It was also there that seeds of cooperation and peacemaking were planted (How else can nine people get by with one bathroom?).

Carolyn attended Rosedale Bible Institute and later graduated from Eastern Mennonite College (now University) with a B.S. in nursing. In 1983, she earned an M.S.N. from the University of Virginia. Along with husband David Schrock-Shenk, Carolyn spent over three years in the Philippines with Mennonite Central Committee. They have two sons, Caleb and John. Carolyn is a member of Community Mennonite Church of Lancaster.

Lawrence E. Ressler, Ph.D., describes himself as "a Mennonite looking for a fight." Lawrence was born in southern Ohio to parents involved in church planting among Appalachian people under the Ohio Conference of the Mennonite Church. Being middle child of seven and growing up Mennonite among non-Mennonites taught Lawrence that there is more than one side to life.

Lawrence is Professor of Social Work and Associate MSW Director at Roberts Wesleyan College in Rochester, New York, where he has worked since 1995. He has had twenty years of experience as social worker, family counselor, and mediator. Lawrence has degrees in social work from Eastern Mennonite University, Temple University, and Case Western Reserve University. He was introduced to practical peacemaking in 1983 through Mennonite Conciliation Service mediation training. Lawrence has been president of the North American Association of Christians in Social Work (NACSW) for six years. He is married to Sharon Martin and has three teenage children.

CPSIA information can be obtained at www.ICGtesting.com
Printed in the USA
BVOW031653301111

277072BV00005B/5/P